GETTING MARRIED AGAIN

GETTING MARRIED AGAIN

by

Susan Fields

DODD, MEAD & COMPANY

NEW YORK

Library of Congress Cataloging in Publication Data

Fields, Susan.
  Getting married again.

  1. Wedding etiquette. 2. Remarriage. I. Title.
BJ2065.R44F5   395'.22   75–6998
ISBN 0–396–07133–3

for Michael

Contents

CHAPTER 1

❀

Making the Decision

If you're planning to get married for the second time, probably you have already run head-on into a painful paradox: all the world may love a lover, but nobody likes a loser—not even the losers themselves.

A second marriage means there must have been a first, and many of your potential well-wishers will choose to view the past as prologue, the beginning of an eventual chain of disasters. Even if you find yourself in your present position through some tragedy other than divorce, you'll encounter resentment when you show signs of crawling out of the pigeonhole people have assigned you to. And you don't have to be Jackie Kennedy—it's true for anyone.

When you get to the point where you feel a talk with someone in your church—if you have one—is necessary, you'll discover that at least half the clergy in America believe that the second marriage, if it is to be countenanced at all, should be accomplished without their benefit or blessing.

You may even fall into the trap yourself. Some of our present mores, especially in the area of matrimony, de-

9

scend virtually unchanged from prehistory. Even though they may not color your own views directly, it's easy and natural to take at least some of our self-esteem from the attitudes of those around us.

That's the reason for this book.

At this critical time in your life, when the Capulets are no more help than the Montagues and you are beginning to feel that it's the two of you against the rest of the entire world, it should help you to have the facts. And it should also help to know you're not alone.

For example, one out of every seven people you pass on the street is already in a second marriage. That's a long way ahead of most minorities.

And did you know that the chances for failure are almost four times greater in the first marriage than they are the second time around? Which means, ironically, that second-timers as a group possess significantly more stability than first-timers: they're older, certainly they have more experience, and they recognize many of the pitfalls. I say "ironically" because you'd have a hard time arriving at these conclusions if your only guide were the popular attitude.

In fact, the second marriage is emerging as one of our culture's most steadfast institutions. And its popularity is increasing at about the same pace as America's skyrocketing rate of divorce. The Department of Health, Education and Welfare has recently found that nine out of ten divorces lead to second marriages. And that same percentage—90%—stays together for the rest of their lives, once they enter the safe haven of a second marriage. Given time, the popular attitude will have to change as well.

Certainly some fairly dramatic alterations have already taken place. Despite the traditions and folklore that still surround first marriages—or perhaps because of them—several of America's leading social thinkers now believe that marriage is too important and too risky to be entrusted to neophytes. Margaret Mead, for example, has spoken of a "trial marriage" in which young couples can make their mistakes without suffering the stigma of public failure. (Few ideas have fallen on more fertile ground judging by the numbers who have apparently embraced Dr. Mead's suggestion.) In the long run, such a concept could have the effect of elevating the second marriage to a position of higher social acceptability than the first.

So when you finally make the decision to go ahead with it, you deserve to be happy and confident that your future will be more fulfilling and more successful than your past. And you may hold your head high. After all, in forming a new family unit, you are helping to repair and strengthen the basic bond that holds our society together.

Besides, you can take it from a recent expert on the subject: marriage is a lot better the second time around.

Of course, people are too pragmatic to spend much time thinking about the impact of their marriage—first, second, or tenth—on society as a whole. On the contrary, most of us might better question what impact society will have on us. But there are plenty of good reasons to get married again, regardless of whether it benefits the rest of the world.

First of all, marriage enables us to greatly multiply the pleasures of this earth by sharing them with those we love. It provides the chance to relate deeply to others, to enhance experience, even to create life. Marriage responds to the proper cultivation, returning more abundant harvests than any garden—in companionship, humor, sympathy, encouragement, understanding, perspective, affection.

If you've been married before, you know that more than the marriage suffers when such opportunities are neglected; you suffer too. And statistics show that you have learned your lesson well.

How quickly you've learned it may be another matter. Some women and men take a relatively long time looking hard at themselves, readjusting their values, analyzing their weaknesses and mistakes. In many cases, this can create a gap of several years between marriages.

Self-discovery, whether alone or with professional help, is an important part of a productive life. But taken too far, it can lead to a turning inward and to habits of mind and attitude which make your reemergence into the mainstream of life more difficult or even impossible. And there is another danger in postponing a second marriage too long: it's too easy to adjust to simply being single.

If you have lived without a partner for too long, it becomes a hassle to think about doing things with anybody but yourself in mind. What about the jobs of washing his underwear as well as your own, ironing his shirts (if you ever did), finding some place besides the towel rack to hang your pantyhose? How about sharing the closet again after a few years of having it all to yourself? Or making real coffee after several hundred mornings of settling for instant?

Then there's the worst adjustment pitfall of all: how are you going to feel about preparing a good dinner at home when you're dog-tired, when in similar circumstances in the past all you've had to do was toss the kids into the car and head for the nearest McDonald's?

If you like being single better than being married, then by all means stay that way. I'm most assuredly not making a case for being married for its own sake. But there are certain assumptions authors must make about their readership, and one of the assumptions I've had to form about you is that you would rather marry.

So don't wait too long. You'll have enough adjustments to make as it is.

Some people try to back into the second marriage in somewhat the same way Margaret Mead suggests entering the first: they just start living together.

If you have kids, such an arrangement is just plain selfish. And not likely to lead anywhere for either of the partners. For another thing, it's an easy out.

Women need emotional security. Even the most liberated women in the world require it, and they are among the first to admit it. The most commonly cited reasons for entering into an arrangement without social sanction are freedom, convenience, and feelings of protest against the establishment. But essentially these are reasons designed to shield rather than to embrace. I've known very few such relationships—if any—that endure and have always felt their rationale for people who've been married before was really just a mask. It disguised their doubts—from the rest of the world perhaps less successfully than from themselves—as to whether either of them was capable of surviving a more permanent relationship.

A woman, particularly, who has been married once will discover that the world finds it difficult to deal with her as a single person. Once you have been part of a couple for a few years, you find that almost everyone you know comes in pairs as well. If you have children as the result of an earlier marriage, they will long for a father, step or real, to restore the family to normalcy. They need a man to take them to ball games or the beach, to fix their bikes, to give them a feeling of security, to make them know they are loved—and that their mother is loved as well.

There are other good arguments for getting married again, though less romantic than pragmatic. Financially, a woman still has a more difficult time getting along in life than a man. Then, too, you probably have a strong desire to prove that you can still do it, that you can make a man happy, and create a successful life in an area where previously you have failed.

Well, you have a lot going for you. It is an exceptional person who can go through the traumas of divorce without learning a lot about himself or herself and about people in general. The chances are at least ten-to-one that the process has matured you, that it has helped you to discover your faults without the luxury of wallowing in them. Now you know what you have to do to become a better partner.

Since you're more adult, you know yourself better—and presumably you know your partner better also. You have both taken the time necessary to develop a good mutual understanding; if you haven't, you should. Both of you must recognize your differences and determine how to come to terms with them so they won't "get you" next time around. You should both have a thorough conviction that the marriage this time is right for all concerned and each of you should be fully committed to making sure it works.

That means thinking of him first when an issue concerns you both. It means being honest even when it hurts—especially when it hurts. It means staying open to your partner, being certain that neither of you is guilty of cutting the lines of communication.

And finally, it means starting out on the right foot, sure of your decision and wanting to tell the whole world.

❀

CHAPTER 2

Your Engagement

Somehow the term "engagement" has never become particularly popular in the context of second marriages, although it applies with exactly the same relevance as the first time. Perhaps it too easily inspires a vision of blushes and giggles, of an earlier innocence that seemed to start unraveling even as you walked away from the altar those many years ago.

Well, let's bring the engagement back into the lexicon of the second-timer and give it the attention it deserves!

Your engagement can be a far more important prelude this time than it was the first. And promises made in the wisdom gained from experience are no less honorable or relevant than those made in the naiveté of youth.

For one thing, this engagement will mean a lot more than before, because it most likely affects a closer circle of family and friends . . . starting with the children.

Of course it is the children—at least those who will become a part of your new household—who should be the first to hear of your big decision. Each parent should take the responsibility for informing his or her offspring. How you do this is more a matter of the individual family situation than of protocol, but several fairly common circumstances are worth a mention here.

If you presently have custody of your children by the previous marriage, you should sit down with them—without your fiancé—and tell them what you plan for the family. The chances are good that they will be excited and happy for you. They may even say, as mine did, "It's about time." You know enough about kids by now to realize that they want you to be happy just as much as they want happiness for themselves.

If they react negatively to the news, have enough character not to just let it go at that. Talk to them. Listen to their fears and apprehensions. Find out what makes them uncertain or fearful. Above all, see it through with them, even in those rare instances where that means enlisting professional guidance. The breaking up of a home is a trauma for all concerned, but never more than for the children. The bringing together of a new family unit should have exactly the opposite effect—and it's your responsibility as a parent to see that it does.

Whatever their reaction, the thing all children need to hear next is that they are still and will always be the most important people in your whole life and in all the world.

Don't worry that this news is going to cause them to infer any slighting of your love for the person you are about to marry. Kids are smarter than most adults in that respect: they know that where love is concerned, superlatives are simply guarantees of parity.

Then you can tell them of your love for the person you are going to marry—that he wants to come and love them too, and that together all of you will build a happy family. Tell them that both of you need their help in making it happen. Reaffirming their position in your life and future plans is most important.

As for children by a previous marriage *not* in your custody and who will *not* be full-time members of the new family unit, how and when you tell them your news will depend on circumstance—not the least element of which is your present relationship with your previous mate.

The next people to tell are your parents: first the bride's, then his. This time the formality of the girl's father giving his daughter's hand in troth is no longer relevant—the woman is now her own person, and the only one who speaks for her legally or otherwise is herself. But certainly you still want both sets of parents to give their blessing, and accordingly you should plan a personal visit in order to impart the news.

You may find that parents are not quite as resilient about these things as your children. First of all, they're a lot older. Second, they are anxious to have you avoid another situation in which you could be hurt again. They may take a dim view of your decision, regardless of how they feel about either of you as individuals. I know cases where one or both sets of parents greeted the announcement of engagement with real horror—perhaps fearful of community or religious condemnation, or a sense of impropriety—even though they genuinely liked and approved of the person their child was planning to marry.

Little can be gained from attempting sidewalk psychoanalysis if this happens, at least insofar as it relates to the causes. It's up to both you and your intended to sit down with both sets of parents and treat them with the same sincerity and compassionate enthusiasm you showed your children. Try to dispel their fears by facing them directly. Tell them how you feel about them and about each other—and let them see for themselves that they are neither losing a son or daughter nor gaining another heartbreak. Let them know that all lines of communication will stay open, and that they should even be improved by the addition of one more good listener.

Honesty and openness with parents will go far in the weeks ahead to ease all of you through the rigors of convention. Do whatever seems appropriate to include them in your plans. The groom's mother, for example, may possess a fund of knowledge about dress styles and colors which the prospective bride would be foolish—and reckless—to leave untapped. Perhaps the groom would enjoy having his father serve as best man, a common honor in such circumstances. Anything that truly demonstrates that you care about your parents, that their experience and feelings matter to you, will serve in the long run to make your own relationship a fuller and happier one.

But it may take some time for one or even both sets

of parents to come around. Eventually, however, when they have seen enough evidence that each of you is good for the other and can create a self-fulfilling family, you'll find they see things your way. So don't make the mistake of giving up with them before they've had all the time they need.

As for how you inform the rest of the world, the second engagement is a bit different. Generally, couples marrying for the second time choose not to announce their engagement in the newspapers. On the other hand, if the bride's parents feel such an announcement is appropriate, it should be simple and along the following format:

> Mr. and Mrs. John Pinto of Pine Street, Duxbury, announce the engagement of their daughter, Mary Pinto Jones (i.e., first name, maiden name, married name) to Mr. James Smith of Plymouth. A fall wedding (or whenever) is planned.

The local society column will probably run such an announcement as a matter of course, although you are not likely to achieve headlines in the major city dailies. The object of the announcement is simply to advise friends of the parents and the betrothed, not to make news.

Engagement parties and gifts are seldom given for the second-time bride. Such rites mark the passage of our youth, a condition most of us have presumably outgrown. However, either set of parents may wish to give a small dinner to introduce you to friends or relatives you may not have met. Such a party could also be hosted by the brother or sister of the prospective couple.

Of course, you each will want to tell your own friends and associates. And this should be handled much as any other piece of important news, either by personal contact or a brief note.

The most widely recognized symbol of betrothal in our culture is, of course, the engagement ring. And there's no reason this marriage should be without one: if you want such a symbol, you should have it. If you had one before, you will most likely look for something a bit different this time, however, and you will probably want to share equally in the selection with your mate. My own engagement ring, for example, was designed by my fiancé and myself, so we both felt that we participated together in the symbolic as well as the literal design of our future marriage. Since we were both born on the same day in the same month, the ring's design takes this marvelous coincidence into account. And I love it all the more for our caring.

CHAPTER 3

❀

Planning the Second Wedding

The second wedding is in many ways more personal than the first, more the creation of the bride and groom. By the same token, it belongs less to the traditions and pomp that sometimes are associated with first weddings. You would do well to avoid confusing the two events.

Where elaborately formal ceremonies are commonplace with first weddings, this time they are as inappropriate as a white bridal gown. Certainly that does not rule out all formality, but it usually precludes being married in a cathedral or two-stepping down the aisle to the strains of the Vienna Boys' Choir.

However, this should in no way constrain the imagination you bring to the second nuptial. On the contrary, there are certain beneficial changes in the degree of freedom you will find in planning your rites this time, even if your earlier wedding was not long ago.

First of all, you're running the show yourselves. You may be wise enough to solicit the advice and consent of your elders on both sides of the family, but all the important decisions—including veto power—are yours alone. That means you'll be putting more of yourselves

into the ceremony, making it inevitably more mean-
ingful.

Maybe this new freedom means you'll be married in a
field of daisies. Or maybe it means that you will not be
married in a field of daisies. The site can range from the
garden of your future home (how many first-timers have
the slightest idea what their real future home will look
like, much less whether it will have a garden?) to a favorite place in the woods, a rock at seaside or a tiny,
medieval chapel in the country. Almost anything goes,
providing it has the approval of your clergyman or
whomever you've chosen to perform the ceremony.

CHOICES

As before, of course, your options this time still include being married simply and quickly in a civil ceremony at city hall . . . or wherever your state and munici-
pality decree such ceremonies be performed. Such a
wedding meets all the legal requirements, though it lacks
romance. But maybe this no-nonsense approach is just
the start your new life needs most. As I say, the choice
is all yours.

One of the first decisions you will have to make is
when to get married: the general time of year, and then
a specific date. The prime consideration will be personal, but of course it may depend on the time of year
you become engaged. Unless you're planning a civil ceremony, you will find that two or three months are re-

quired for completion of all the necessary arrangements for even a simple wedding. You will also learn that there are certain seasons or dates, such as Christmas or (in some churches) Lent, when marriages are not allowed. So your two principal caveats with respect to timing are local custom and religious tradition. Your town clerk and pastor are the best sources for this information.

Considerations of timing also relate to the hour of day. In the South, evening weddings are considered fashionable, while in the East there is a bias toward afternoon ceremonies. Probably the best guide in this respect is the convenience of all concerned, especially if travel is involved. When family members are coming from a considerable distance, you should decide—perhaps with their concurrence—whether the ceremony will be more enjoyable and less fatiguing on the afternoon of the day they arrive or the morning of the day after. And it also depends on what you plan to do after the ceremony: what kind of reception is planned, and what are your own travel arrangements, if any?

CHURCH AND CLERGY

If you decide that a church wedding is in order, both partners face some familiar problems and some that will be new. When two religions are involved, you will have to determine whether a joint ceremony is permissible, and you and your fiancé will then have to work out where to hold the wedding. Naturally you will have to discuss the matter with both sets of clergy. All else being equal, however, the choice of church usually rests with the bride.

One of the new factors you'll discover on talking to the clergy is that churches take differing attitudes with regard to second marriages. Which means a different set of rules. The church may take the view that you are still married to your first mate—even in cases where he or she is already happily remarried and living an entirely separate life. As a general rule, for example, Roman Catholic clergy require proof of annulment as well as of divorce before they will consider a second marriage ceremony. There are exceptions, and the Roman Catholic church has been moving through historical changes in this and other respects, so every reader is encouraged to determine the present position by direct consultation wth his local pastor. (State rules are also quickly changing concerning the minimum time lapse between marriages.) And there are religions in which not even widowhood is sufficient basis for a second marriage.

Assuming you'll find a proper solution to the religious aspects of your own special case, there are some documents which clergy often request. In addition to the possibility that you will both be asked for certificates of baptism, confirmation, or other proof of church membership, it is not uncommon for the priest, minister, or rabbi to demand as well a copy of your divorce decree. A letter from the rector or parson of the other partner's church attesting to his or her marital status may also be required. Some churches, especially in the case of a mixed marriage, insist on a short period of religious instruction before the wedding is permitted.

Whatever date you finally select, advance reservations are imperative with both the church and the clergyman. This is especially true in the spring months, most notably June. Some churches are committed as much as a year in advance for June weekends.

The clergyman will suggest numerous other details before your meeting with him, and you and your fiancé should discuss these privately in advance. If another cleric is to participate in the service, permission will have to be obtained from the pastor of the church in which the wedding is held. Permission may also be required from the second cleric's church as well. This may not come automatically, so be prepared for delay or disappointment.

Details less complex but still important include the choice of music, floral arrangements, rehearsal schedules, seating plans, parking arrangements for the wedding party. If the clergyman doesn't supply this information himself, then it may be that these latter considerations fall within the province of a church sexton or the pastor's secretary. But do ask.

Regarding the music, if this involves more than an organist, you will want to rehearse the soloist before you rehearse the ceremony itself. The rehearsal needn't take place at the church, but you should run through it all at least once, and a piano is a poor substitute for the organ accompanist.

When you and your fiancé discuss the clergyman's fee (it's the best man's job, but the groom's money) be sure to give equal amounts to both clerics if two should officiate. And don't be afraid to ask the rate. (Most clergymen expect some kind of "thank offering" to the church if not to themselves. Even if they deny it vigorously or simply state, "Oh, just say a prayer for me," pay something.) If you can't settle the price in advance, then from $25 to $50 is acceptable, depending on the simplicity of the service.

When the best man gives the clergyman the money, it should be delivered in a plain envelope, either check or cash, and should be given to the cleric after the ceremony has been completed. The best man should avoid the temptation to conduct this transaction with the same sleight of hand he might reward a headwaiter. This is not a tip, but rather payment for services rendered.

The particular rules and rites of religions vary widely, of course, and there is no hope of listing them all here. But what we can do is offer a brief synopsis of what we've discovered to be generally true as of this writing. However, make sure you seek the advice of a current authority in your own church.

AT THE MOMENT

Most Protestant churches will allow remarriage of their members under certain conditions. The Episcopal

Church normally permits divorced persons to remarry when the minister involved recommends this to be sound. The Bishop's final approval is then usually forthcoming. (Be sure you're up to the minute on the latest laws governing time between marriages.)

The Roman Catholic Church as a rule will not allow the marriage of divorced persons unless there has been a special canonical annulment by a church court. In some sections of the country, however, local bishops will occasionally permit divorced persons to be married; this is still rare, but it may become more general soon and is well worth an inquiry of your local pastor.

The churches of the *Eastern Rite, Greek and Russian Orthodox,* do permit remarriage of those who have received religious decrees of divorce or annulment. Note that a religious decree and a civil decree are distinctly different and should not be confused.

In the *Jewish* faith, significant differences between the Orthodox and Reform branches are seen with special clarity in their attitudes toward remarriage. Orthodox and Conservative rabbis do not recognize any divorce except that granted by religious decree. Most Reform rabbis, on the other hand, do recognize civil divorce and will perform a second marriage . . . unless it is a mixed marriage, in which case they will not.

NONDENOMINATIONAL AND NONRELIGIOUS

If your religion is one that does not permit remarriage in the church, or if you and your fiancé are not members of a particular congregation, don't give up. There are still steps to be taken if you are among the many people who just won't feel married unless the wedding takes place in a church.

First of all, you might consider a nondenominational chapel, of which there are many throughout the country. Often these chapels are located in places of particular historic or scenic value. In Sudbury, Massachusetts, for example, there is a lovely Colonial church connected with Longfellow's famed Wayside Inn; people come to be married from miles around, making arrangements through the Inn but providing their own clergy or other official. A cleric does not necessarily have to officiate for you to be married in a church under such circumstances.

Similarly, many denominational churches allow strangers to rent their facilities for a small fee. Just make sure in advance that there is no church rule against the re-marriage of divorced people.

I know one couple who were married by a ship's captain and a Justice of the Peace on a lake excursion boat. The ship's captain had no authority at all, but the Justice of the Peace did and the ceremony was perfectly legal. And it satisfied this couple's need for the combination of tradition as well as individuality.

Garden weddings can also provide a lovely tradition in an attractive setting without being upset by religious rules or limitations. These cannot be planned with the same degree of certainty as a wedding indoors, however;

the tent has not yet been built that won't leak in a rainstorm.

Four Types of Ceremony

Basically, there are four different types of second-time wedding ceremonies to choose from:

1. Church or chapel, either semi-formal or informal, but never formal
2. Home wedding
3. Outdoor or garden
4. Civil ceremony

... AND THE MONEY QUESTION

In addition to the religious and traditional guidelines already discussed, you may well be influenced by financial considerations. The first time, the bride usually receives a substantial subsidy from her parents toward the costs of the wedding—perhaps even the entire expense. But you can't expect that to happen again. You may be blessed with particularly generous parents, still it's not something the average second-timer can rely on unless the offer is made in advance. Under no circumstances should the parents be asked.

This is a situation—one among many—that demands open discussion with your fiancé. There is a tradition requiring the bride to pay, but that consideration is certainly subordinate to more prosaic elements, such as who can afford what. After all, in practical fact your joint resources are involved regardless of from whose bank account you take the money. In the first marriage the groom never helps, but in the second marriage he often does. Talk it over.

CHURCH OR CHAPEL

Money may well determine the choice you finally make. *A semi-formal* church or chapel wedding is about as elaborate as you can be within the conventions of a second marriage, and this usually costs the most. You may mark off the front pews with a small ribbon, signifying their use by close relatives, but ordinarily no aisle ribbons, aisle carpets, or canopy are used. At most, you will have two or three attendants each—perhaps a maid or matron of honor and two children for the bride, and a best man and two ushers for the groom. The guest list should be kept under 75, though more can attend the reception. Such services are usually held in the afternoon or evening.

Informal church or chapel weddings, on the other hand, are most often scheduled for the morning or afternoon, and seldom in the evening. There are no attendants in the conventional sense, although two legal witnesses are usually required to sign the marriage certificate. Such witnesses may be designated maid or matron of honor and best man, but that's purely a matter of who they are and what you think of them. Decorations are minimal or may be dispensed with entirely, at most a few flowers and a little greenery. The service involves no processional or music although there might be music at the reception. Guests may be greeted by the bride's parents and other relatives before the ceremony, but there is neither formal seating nor ushers.

At *both* semi-formal and informal weddings in churches and chapels, the groom enters with the minister, and the best man, if there is one. At the informal service, the groom's parents will also stand in front of the minister, though slightly to the rear of their son, permitting space for the bride when she enters. The bride's mother next takes a similar position near where her daughter will be standing. The bride then enters, with her matron of honor if she has one, and the marriage is performed. After the bride and groom kiss, the guests and family offer their best wishes as well, without waiting for the couple to leave the church.

HOME WEDDINGS

Home weddings are the most popular for second marriages. Usually small, they may be either semi-formal or informal; most often the latter. They may involve either religious or civil services, but bear in mind that both require advance planning with whomever you choose to officiate. The reasons for their popularity are readily apparent. They're economical; they afford a good "out" for keeping guest lists manageable; and they're a tasteful, familiar alternative when there is still a residue of community rancor over past events (especially when that rancor precludes a church service). A final obvious reason is the weather; you can't get married in the garden when it's raining or snowing, and a warm fireplaced livingroom may be just the thing.

Depending on the type of wedding planned, you may want to leave your home just as it is—or you can bring in a kneeling bench and temporary altar, plus two banks of rented chairs divided by flowers, greens, and ribbons as in a church. Either way, you will probably want some flowers. The bride's mother (or matron of honor) ordinarily serves as hostess, seating guests and showing the cleric where to dress. The entrance for the wedding itself is essentially the same as a chapel ceremony: groom and best man walk in first with clergyman, then the bride's mother—perhaps with an usher or male relative—followed by the bridesmaids, then matron of honor. The bride walks in alone and stands at the groom's side. The ceremony ends the same way as an informal chapel wedding. The bride and groom may then lead the wedding party to the refreshments.

OUTDOOR OR GARDEN

The outdoor or garden wedding seldom differs from the home service except that it can occasionally be larger or more formal, depending on individual preference. As in a house, your choice of setting will be related to convenience, attractiveness, and space. You may choose a processional to the altar, but the party then leaves it just as they leave a wedding in the home. If the guest list is sufficiently large, you may want to form a reception line after the ceremony, but that too is optional. Even if you are certain of the weather, a canopy of some kind is strongly recommended; ice lasts longer—and so do the guests—if they have some refuge from the sun.

CIVIL

Conventions governing civil ceremonies vary from place to place. To some extent these depend on whether the official is a judge, a registrar, a clerk, or justice of the peace; each can advise you of his own limitations and requirements. The setting may be designated by law (e.g., judge's chambers or registrar's office), or you may choose to hold the ceremony in a private home, hotel, club, public hall, or even a privately rented chapel. Chapel weddings need not, necessarily, be religious as long as you're certain that such an arrangement is in keeping with the rules of the organization from which the chapel is rented. As in any wedding ceremony, two legal witnesses are required. These can be two friends—whom you may designate as best man and maid/matron of honor or complete strangers who are known to the official performing the marriage. The bride should wear a street dress and the groom a business suit; the bridal bouquet is waived in favor of a corsage. The official's fee, usually set by him in advance, is traditionally from $10 to $30. This should be presented to him in a plain envelope, and with the same tact as one would pay a minister or priest, once the ceremony is completed. If the official for some reason waives his fee—perhaps because you're friends—then a prompt note of gratitude is in order, as well as some small token of your thanks. And certainly in such circumstances the official should be invited to any celebration that follows the ceremony.

RINGS

One other detail that should be decided well in advance of the wedding is the choice of ring for the bride —and, if it is to be a double ring ceremony, for the groom as well. Although the engagement ring is often selected separately, their designs should be compatible, assuming that you decided to have an engagement ring in the first place. The bride's rings should both be of the same metal, whether platinum or white or yellow gold. The groom ordinarily would wear a plain band of yellow gold, but variations are not uncommon, white gold being the most popular alternative. In addition to her engagement and wedding rings, the bride might choose to wear a guard ring as well, particularly where it provides the double function of protecting the stone-bearing engagement ring and acting as an interface between it and the wedding band; sometimes the guard ring forms a Chinese lock, combining all three bands into a single unit when worn.

Fitting the ring doesn't take long, but if adjustments are required they can run into several days. Likewise, the inscription on the wedding band(s) can be time-consuming, so plan well in advance. The groom usually words the inscription, inasmuch as the ring is his gift to the bride, but that shouldn't rule out your both contributing to the authorship of the sentiment—especially in double-ring ceremonies where the same legend will appear on both bands.

If you're at a loss for the proper sentiment, or if you're simply not the type, your inscription can follow the time-honored practice of listing the bride's maiden initials (not the first-marriage initials), followed by the groom's initials and the date of your wedding.

The rings are entrusted to the chief attendants just before the ceremony: the best man holds the groom's, and the maid/matron of honor takes responsibility for the bride's.

CHAPTER 4

❀

The Bridal Party:
Who Does What

Regardless of the kind of ceremony you decide on, the number of people you invite to your second wedding is likely to be smaller than the number attending a similar ceremony the first time around. Similarly, the size of the bridal party will be smaller as well. But the fact that the number of participants is smaller in no way diminishes the importance of their roles.

Whether you are planning a civil service in a judge's chambers or a semi-formal ceremony in a church, you will still require at least two attendants. The extent of their responsibilities and the number of additional attendants will be determined by the size and style of wedding.

For civil ceremonies and informal church weddings, the two witnesses required by law will probably be your best man and maid/matron of honor, who will sign your marriage certificate. If you elect a semi-formal ceremony, you may want to add an usher or two (if you expect over thirty guests), as well as a bridesmaid and/or flower girl.

These latter assignments are an ideal means by which to bring the children into the new marriage, but you should be aware—as probably you already are—that many authorities on etiquette maintain that the children should be the last to know, and by no means be permitted to attend or participate in either parent's remarriage. Okay—but what do you tell them when you get home?

That attitude, fortunately, belongs to an earlier era. The reason such advice persists in our own age is that the so-called arbiters of how we should act toward one another are really just historians, and they are fighting a losing battle against change. Happily, our own time is one where human needs weigh more heavily than an abstract sense of decorum. By all means, include the children.

Besides setting a very positive tone for all concerned, they will love the fun of being involved. Young boys from six on up make wonderful ushers, and you'll be surprised how well-behaved and serious they become when the actual moment arrives. Some of your best wedding photographs are bound to include Great Aunt Sally entering the church on the arm of your son or stepson. Your daughter may attend you if she is over twelve, but if she is younger she probably would feel more comfortable as a junior bridesmaid or flower girl. (Flower girls are usually eight or under.) No less an authority than Amy Vanderbilt argued vehemently that your children should not even attend the wedding—so be guided accordingly.

As for who does what, and when, I suggest the following:

THE BRIDE

The bride is the central figure in any wedding. But this time she has an obligation to conduct herself with seriousness and maturity; after all, one is no longer a child bride, and it would be unbecoming to giggle, simper, or gush. Instead, you should make it clear by your demeanor that you recognize the important implications of the step you are taking, and that you greet it with joy and dignity.

By the time of the wedding, you will have already taken care of most of the preparatory details, perhaps with the help and/or consultation of your mother, assuming that she is willing. These matters include responsibility for planning the dress of the entire wedding party, arranging all aspects of the reception, collaboration with the groom on the style of the wedding, the actual ceremony itself (including the wording of the rites, if you have a special preference or wish to personalize the vows), the choice of flowers, selection of music, designation of musicians, invitations and announcements, and overall timing. You will want to have gifts for your attendants and for your future husband, and you will presumably have made a head start on some of the thank-you notes for the gifts which you and your husband will have received. No difference, so far, from the routine of the first time.

If your first marriage ended in divorce, however, you have the additional requirement of producing a copy of the decree, since this must be attached to your license when you apply for it. If you and the groom are from different towns, you will need two copies. And if he has been married and divorced as well, you will also need a copy or copies of this document.

THE GROOM

Probably by now, some role-conscious couple has decided to reverse the traditional hierarchy implied by the usual wedding announcement, and refer to themselves as the groom and bride. But saying it doesn't make it so: the groom is still distinctly Number Two in the normal order of things related to weddings, no matter how briefly he must yield the primacy he enjoys in most other mortal matters.

The successful bride, however, would be ill-advised to belabor her brief advantage, just as the husband would be foolish to make too much of any imbalance that prevails thereafter.

In fact, it should be a challenge to the bride to be certain that the groom's role is less passive than custom decrees. The second wedding provides unusual opportunities for male participation. Of course, the bride and groom work much closer in planning the wedding itself —more than the first time, when the bride is far likelier to defer to the wishes of her mother than to those of her future husband. This is not because first-time brides are more selfish, but simply because their mothers habitually play larger roles in their lives, and that habit has been institutionalized in the veto powers society has given mothers in first marriages. By the second marriage, however, that habit has been broken and the veto powers have long since disappeared.

The groom will work with the bride in planning the type of wedding, in defining the terms—and perhaps the language—of the ceremony, in deciding who will be invited, to whom announcements will be sent, how the party will dress. He has the sole vote on his best man and ushers, if any, but as with most other matters he will doubtless want to talk it over with the bride.

Under no circumstance should the bride try to select the best man. This may sound idiotically obvious, but I know several instances where this transgression has occurred, and it's no way to start a new life. The bride who follows that particular folly is likely to be faced with the choice again and again.

The groom, like the bride, is responsible for a gift for his partner, and for his best man and for each of the ushers. He is also expected to advise all members on his side of the wedding party just what to wear, when to show up, and what they're supposed to do when they get there. Typically, the groom's gifts are monogrammed belt buckles or some other accessory jewelry such as a tie clip or cuff links; the monogram is the recipient's, of course, not the bride and groom's. His gift to the bride can be just about anything except food or wearing apparel.

The same requirements pertain to the groom as to the bride if he too has been married previously. Copies of the divorce decree must be appended to all license applications.

Traditionally, the groom takes responsibility for getting blood tests done in time, obtaining the license, and making all arrangements for the honeymoon. Even these details are likely to become more cooperative projects in the second wedding, however, and the only rules that need apply are those of mutual convenience and common sense.

MAID/MATRON OF HONOR

Before the wedding, there is no special assignment for the bride's chief attendant except that she help out in whatever ways she can—perhaps with sending out the announcements, taking care of the kids, or just pouring hot coffee as you all come into the home stretch. Most first-time brides choose their closest friends for this honor; sometimes that means the bride's sister or future sister-in-law. The criteria are the same the second time. It is unlikely that a bride would assign the responsibility to a daughter by the previous marriage—unless widowed

—and even less likely if divorced and that daughter were herself not an adult at the time of the second wedding. In the latter case, the daughter would appear to have sided with her mother over her father, which would be tasteless and cruel to all concerned, especially to the daughter. Ordinarily, you would not choose the same honor attendant you had the first time, especially in a religious ceremony where the marriage is a sacrament in which all members participate as witnesses and guarantors.

The maid/matron of honor usually assembles her own wedding outfit and pays for everything except her flowers, although it is not unreasonable for the bride and groom to take on some of the expense themselves if the honor will otherwise cause an excessive financial burden on the recipient.

This bride's chief attendant has the responsibility for showing the clergyman where to vest in a home wedding, and of course she acts as an official witness for purposes of the law, signing your marriage certificate. She helps dress the bride, leads her into the church, holds her flowers during the ceremony, and follows the married couple out, usually beside the best man. If there is going to be a receiving line, she will stand on the right side of the groom, and if there is a wedding table afterward, she will sit at the groom's left. Her last duty is to help the bride make her getaway with the groom; this usually includes laying out the outfit that will be worn on the honeymoon, assisting in the change after the wedding or reception, marshalling the kids (whether the children have participated in the ceremony or were merely honored guests), and making sure that the last-minute necessities have been packed.

Best Man

The best man is usually just that: the husband's best friend or closest male relative. It is not uncommon for a groom to ask his father to be best man—but it would be inappropriate for the groom to ask his own son by a previous marriage, especially if the groom's former wife is still living, unless the son is over 21, an adult, and can make his own decision without nurturing the guilt or anxiety that might attach to "siding" with one natural parent "against" another. The groom does not use the same best man in this wedding as in his first.

The best man's most visible duty, beyond making sure the groom shows up and carrying a ring, is to offer the first toast after the ceremony. The less noted functions are similar to those of his female counterpart: seeing that the groom has both shoes on and that his tie is fixed properly, witnessing the ceremony with his signature on the marriage certificate, preceding the groom into the church, and following the couple out. He is also supposed to make sure the ushers are aware of their duties, dressed properly, and on time. It is the best man who presents the clergyman his fee, although the money is the groom's; again, a plain white envelope is used to blunt the imputation of commerce to either party.

The toast can be anything appropriate to the best interests of the bride and groom—health, wealth, and happiness are safe wishes. Lots of guidebooks offer standard remarks for such occasions, but the best man would do better simply to speak whatever is in his heart. If he isn't very good on his feet, that's all right too; a brief statement that means what it says is a lot better than a flowery one that doesn't.

Along with being valedictorian, the best man has to watch out that no one plays any serious practical jokes on the wedding party at the reception. In a second marriage, the prime suspects for such activities are the children. One way to defuse potential embarrassment is for the best man to help the would-be pranksters direct their energies and enthusiasms to more productive and acceptable forms of expression, such as decorating the escape car. Perhaps he can supply a can of foam shaving cream and a few rolls of streamers and tape, plus the usual tin cans and old shoes. The kids will love it, and it should keep them all out of trouble.

As the chief bridal attendant, the best man's final job is to make sure the couple enjoys a smooth getaway. This means more than just helping the groom change into streetwear once the reception is over. The best man may be given responsibility for getting the packed bags safely locked into the honeymoon car (or checked on the proper airline or train), and he may be expected to drive the couple away from the reception. If tickets, large amounts of money, keys, passports, or other valuables are involved, the best man may also be given these for safe keeping until the last minute. Last minutes are famous for confusion and forgetfulness, so the best man had better be certain he discharges all the tasks entrusted him; a checklist is recommended. One document traditionally in his custody until the very end is the marriage certificate. The time is long behind us when a couple needs such a document to check into a bridal suite, but if you plan a honeymoon outside the United States, you may want that piece of paper to prove you have the right to get off the plane.

USHERS

The only real function of the usher is to usher. Presumably anyone who can get as far as the church under his or her own power is able to make it down the aisle to a pew without help, so this assignment is largely honorary and often dispensable. In weddings with less than thirty guests, for example, ushers are not required. If the couple is looking for a good way to recognize close friends or relations who missed being best man, however, the role of usher is perfect. For second marriages, it's also a good way to bring the kids into the act.

The ushers report to the best man, but if the party is of any size, the groom or best man usually designate a head usher who is responsible for keeping track of the others. All are supposed to dress the same way: the formal wedding apparel is rented at their own expense, with the groom picking up the cost of neckwear, gloves, and boutonnieres. For the sake of uniformity, the groom (perhaps with the help of his best man) will sometimes make arrangements with a single supplier of men's wear so that everyone has a reasonable hope of appearing as if they're all members of the same wedding. This is especially good advice in a time when fashions for men are changing so quickly and in such dramatic ways.

The look-alikes assemble at the back of the church about an hour before the ceremony to greet the arrivals. Friends of the bride are seated on the left, the groom's friends on the right (right and left as seen from the back of the church). The ushers use the rotation method, but in cases where they are particular friends with an arriving guest, they are allowed to break the sequence and escort that person out of order. A discreet amount of small talk is encouraged, but in subdued tones—though of course not once the ceremony has started, should a guest be thoughtless enough to arrive late.

The usual manner is for the usher to extend his right elbow for the support of the arriving ladies. Even if a lady comes with her husband, which is not unreasonable at this type of affair, the gentleman is expected to defer graciously to convention, following a few steps behind the usher and his wife. If a man arrives alone, the usher has the option of walking along with him or sending him on his way; certainly in cases where the single male is nearly blind with grief, then the humane thing is for the usher to guide him at least part way.

Once the church has begun to fill, the ushers need not be as fastidious about the side on which late guests are seated. In a second wedding this is not likely to happen, but you may have decided on a particularly small chapel and, as it approaches capacity, the ushers may balance the distribution so that no one is stuck too far in the back.

The head usher usually accompanies the mother of the bride and the mother of the groom—but if one of the other ushers is a brother or son of the bride or groom, then he should perform the honor instead. When several ladies arrive at once, the oldest goes first.

Once the wedding ceremony is over, the ushers are expected to participate in the recessional, helping the mothers and/or other ladies of station down the aisle. Although they are not included in the receiving line (nor is the best man), the ushers generally share the bridal table at the reception. They have the option of proposing additional toasts after the best man has led off, but it is not an obligation.

There are usually two major differences between a first wedding usher and his counterpart in the second: at the second wedding he is likely to be either older or younger (because he is the groom's peer or his son), and he is less likely to be such a delight to the bridesmaids (because he is probably married himself or too young to be eligible).

BRIDESMAIDS, JUNIOR BRIDESMAIDS, FLOWER GIRLS

Bear in mind that this is your second wedding, and a formal ceremony is out. If you decide on a semi-formal wedding, the size of the affair is going to be smaller than an equivalent function the first time around. This means the size of the wedding party will be smaller as well.

Now that I've emphasized that again . . . here's the other side of the coin. Additional bridal attendants add color and fun to the occasion, they don't have much in the way of responsibility, and it's certainly a good way to bring in the kids.

If you decide that's the way you want to go, the bride and groom are responsible for assembling the wedding outfits (that includes associated costs—but if the attendants are your own kids, you'd do this anyway.) You also provide the flowers. The flower girl should avoid strewing rosebuds in your path—first, because it's dangerous, especially under the feet of older members of the party who may follow the recessional down the aisle, and second, because many churches and chapels have rules against this kind of littering. The only difference between a bridesmaid and a junior bridesmaid is age, and you're probably better off without the distinctions. The flower girl is usually under eight years of age. All the attendants, including children, must attend rehearsal.

PARENTS: HIS, HERS

Hopefully, the bride's mother will be willing and able to act as a strong right arm during the weeks before the wedding. She has already been through it all once, which should help make the second time easier for her—but her main contribution will be to lend moral support and encouragement, plus helpful suggestions. If possible, she should meet with the mother of the groom; if not possible, then at least they should be in touch by telephone or letter, congratulating each other on the good match their children have made. This kind of rapport between parents can do much to ease tensions that inevitably arise during the hectic days of planning and preparation.

The bride's mother is the last person to be escorted to her seat before the ceremony starts, and she will be the first to follow the recessional down the aisle when it is over. She will sit in the left front pew (from the back of the church) and will have a place of honor at the reception that follows.

The bride's father plays a less important role in the second wedding than in the first; he has already discharged his responsibility to you once, you are older than the girl he gave away the first time—and therefore presumably more self-sufficient. He has absolutely no moral responsibility—nor any social one—to provide you with anything more than emotional support. If he decides to do more, the decision should be his alone, and should be in all ways consistent with his disposition and ability.

For these reasons, many second-time brides prefer to walk to the altar by themselves. However, if the bride and her father share the sentiment that a repetition of the first wedding tradition is appropriate, then by all means they should make the trip together. And by the same token, the bride's mother may give her away instead. The bride's father will sit with his wife during the ceremony. His dress will be the same as that of the other men in the wedding party.

The groom's parents will be seated in the right front pew, just before the parents of the bride are ushered to their seats. Their attire should be consistent with the formality of the ceremony.

If the children of your previous marriage are not in the ceremony, they should be seated just before their grandmothers and on the proper side.

If one or both sets of parents are deceased, you may choose to honor a very close relative—aunt, grandmother, great uncle—who can participate in the ceremony in their stead. You wouldn't expect any other than purely ceremonial help from whomever you ask, whether they are your parents or not, so the choice is never an onus or a burden.

EXPENSES

The second marriage is accounted in a very different way from the first. Partly this is because the second marriage is removed by one important step and probably several years from the concept of the bridal dowry: while the bride's dowry was given by the father the first time, it is now either in the possession of the bride herself or no longer exists, a casualty of the first marriage. But dowry aside, the difference in the view of responsibility between the two events goes deeper than tradition. The commitment you bring to the second marriage is really what's at issue.

For one thing, that commitment is between two mature adults who are responsible for at least their own lives, and very likely for the lives of others as well. The years ahead are not being seen by either of you as the dreamy fantasy of post-adolescence, but rather for exactly what they are likely to be, based on experience and the kind of self-knowledge that has been earned the hard way.

When I refer to the dowry, of course I'm not thinking in terms of goats, geese, and grain any more than I'm suggesting vast estates and family jewels. What I have in mind are the things that many daughters' fathers pay for when the little girl leaves home. Usually these include most of the expenses of the first wedding. But they can also take the form of help with a college education for the husband or wife, a down payment on the first home, maybe some furnishings—it all depends on what's needed and what's possible.

That same consideration—what's needed and what's possible—should govern the second marriage as well. But, of course, this time it is not the bride's father who is making the decisions: it is the bride and groom themselves. And each should contribute from their separate resources whatever they are best able to provide, bearing in mind that in practical fact it makes little difference who really pays—because both of them will share equally, in the long run, in both the expenses and the benefits.

Perhaps it would be remiss of me not to provide a list of the expenses you can anticipate. The following is *not*, however, a guide to either the bride's or groom's respective liability.

Marriage license and blood tests

Engagement ring (hers)

Wedding ring(s)

Divorce decrees (two copies of each)

Death Certificate (if previous marriage ended in death)

Rental of church, chapel, hall, garden, boat, or whatever

Payment of the judge, minister, rabbi, priest, or town clerk

Bride's wedding dress

Dress for bridal attendants, gloves and ties for men

Groom's wedding clothes

Flowers (bride's, flower girl's, boutonnieres for groom and other men in party, corsages for mothers, altar pieces)

Gifts for wedding party members

Photographer

Accommodations for out-of-town members of wedding
    party
Bride's stationery
Liquor, food, service, and space for reception
Rehearsal dinner
Wedding trip

There is only one item the bride and groom each pays
for independently in the second marriage, and that is
their gift to each other.

CHAPTER 5

❀

The Reception

The tradition of a reception following a wedding is just as valid for the second marriage as it was for the first: you have something to celebrate, and you want to share it with your friends and family.

There is an almost unlimited choice as to the form this reception may take. It can be anything from a simple get-together among a few intimates all the way to the full treatment of a semi-formal party. Whichever way you go, or anywhere in between, remember that this time the burden of the expense will be yours. For some couples, whose circumstances and inclinations permit, this may mean that they can spend more—and with a clearer conscience—than before. For others, it may mean pulling in the horns slightly. In the latter case, it sometimes makes better sense to cut down on the extravagance of the catering than to whittle away at the guest list; a smaller dinner steak (or simply chicken) is a perfectly acceptable alternative to a fewer number of participants. Either way, however, be governed by the same judgment and restraint that determined your choice of wedding ceremony. After all, a couple who marries with becoming modesty can still be criticized for overdoing things at the reception.

Whether you decide to go big or small, however, the kind of reception you hold is influenced to some extent by your wedding. If you're married in the morning, a late breakfast or brunch might be appropriate. Similarly, a noon or afternoon ceremony might call for luncheon, a punch party with hors d'oeuvres, or dinner. Whether you decide on sit-down service or a buffet, it is customary to seat the wedding party at a bridal table. And if you're going to hold the reception anywhere near the site of the wedding, all the guests at the wedding should of course be invited. Which doesn't mean you can't invite others to the reception. In fact, small weddings and larger receptions are quite common, particularly when it's not the first marriage for the bride and/or groom.

Unlike invitations to the wedding, those for the reception may be printed in a second marriage. If there are no additional guests at the reception, however, the need for printed invitations is obviated; simply invite them to both functions at once, either verbally or by handwritten note.

If the reception is semi-formal, then any flowers used in the service are commonly arranged around the rooms in which the reception is to be held. Guests and relatives can lend a hand with this kind of decoration, and the reception provides an opportunity for guests to add a bouquet or two of their own, if they so desire.

Often, the reception will begin with a receiving line

. . . but only if the function is semi-formal. Otherwise the couple and the wedding party meet the guests upon completion of the ceremony.

If the reception is semi-formal, there is always some kind of a wedding cake. The cake is optional at any other type of reception, but certainly it's such a tradition that many of the guests will be disappointed not to spot one. Unlike the cake served at first receptions, however, this time you stay away from solid white. A pastel trim takes the edge off the pristine icing and still provides a pleasing and appropriate effect. Another first-wedding convention you should perhaps discard this time is the kewpie couple on top of the cake: of course you can have the bride and groom figures if you want, but it's in better taste to replace them with flowers or some other decoration.

Though dancing is not common at a second marriage reception, the options are yours. It shouldn't be ritualized, however, as it was the first time. Still, some form of music provides a pleasant background. But this can be expensive and is not always easy to arrange. So plan early.

Other details include a photographer, or at least some preparation for having pictures of the reception. If you decide to hire a professional, it will almost certainly be the same one who covers the wedding. An alternative is to rely on snapshots taken by friends and members of the wedding party, but these are never as satisfactory—

and you will always have trouble tracking them all down once the honeymoon is over.

A wedding guest book can also be fun.

There are some rare instances where second weddings are followed by formal receptions, but only under unusual circumstances. If only the groom has been married before, if both the bride and groom have many friends whom they feel should be invited, and if cost is no object, then the following additional elements may be included in the same basic protocol that pertains to semi-formal events.

An announcer attends the reception; his assignment to introduce all the guests by name and relationship, whether relative or friend, to the receiving line.

Formal engraved invitations are sent out for the reception.

There is a bride's table and a parents' table.

Music for dancing.

An elegant menu is served by professionals.

THE RECEIVING LINE

As mentioned earlier, you can have a receiving line whether the reception is formal or semi-formal, but in other circumstances you would normally greet the guests at the wedding itself rather than at the reception. The main reason for having such a procedure at all is self-evident: the guests may not be known to all members of the wedding party, and unless the reception is very small, this is the most straightforward and efficient way to be sure that everyone has a chance to become acquainted.

Both sets of parents may participate in the receiving line if they want to—and usually they do—but any or all of them can be excused if it interferes with some other responsibility they may have at the reception, or if they feel they already know as many of the guests as they care to. Except in rare instances, the parents are not going to be acting as hosts, so this is not their party as much as it was the first time. If you decide to leave them out, it's perfectly appropriate for the bride and groom to receive guests with only the immediate members of the wedding party in the line.

Let's assume the maximum receiving line—which means we are assuming that rare bird, a formal reception. The line would start with the announcer, and would then include the mother of the bride, the father of the groom, the mother of the groom, father of the bride, the bride herself, the groom, maid/matron of honor, and bridesmaids. It would not include the best man or the ushers or the clergyman who officiated, nor any small children.

No matter which members of the above group we eliminate, either because they opt out or because they were never in, the rest of the group simply closes ranks. A common reception line at a semi-formal reception might well include merely the bride, the groom, and the maid/matron of honor.

The receiving line should be near the entrance to the area where the festivities will be taking place, preferably just inside the door. It is the heart of the reception in that it not only provides an opportunity for the bride and groom to accept the best wishes of every guest individually, but it brings the party into one area where they can meet each other and begin the celebration with a minimum of dawdling.

The rule about small children really pertains only to the flower girl. If the bridesmaids include your own children, they should, of course, be encouraged to participate in the receiving line. Besides enjoying it, they'll enchant the crustiest relative, in-law, or guest.

The bride need not hold her flowers, but the maid/ matron of honor and the bridesmaids in the line should keep their bouquets in their left hands through the entire procedure. While they also keep on their hats and gloves, the men do just the opposite.

As the guests go down the line, they are introduced in turn by the last person to meet them. In other words, the bride introduces the guest to the groom, the groom passes the introduction on to the maid/matron of honor. However, if the groom spots an old friend whom the bride has not yet met, it is proper and necessary that he lean around his wife and perform the introduction himself. The line stays together until every guest has passed through. This need not take an unduly long time, as the conversation in such circumstances is always limited to a very few words. Receiving lines are not the place to discuss sports, politics or religion. The bride should be told how beautiful she is, the groom must hear how fortune has smiled on him, the bridesmaids can be flattered or joshed, and the parents, if they stay in the line, ought to be handled with equal parts of sympathy and dispatch.

The point is, keep moving.

WHO SITS WHERE

There are all kinds of variations in the way people arrange their bridal tables. Probably, but not necessarily, your decision will have some relationship to the way in which you set up your receiving line, if you have one. Even more likely, it will be influenced by the facilities where the reception is held.

Your first decision will involve both sets of parents: should they sit at the bridal table, or should they have a table of their own? Still bearing in mind that this reception is not your parents' party, your choice should nevertheless underscore their importance to the event and the esteem in which they are held by their children.

Let's say you decide to include the entire wedding party at one table. If we assume that the reception room has the required tables, space, and flexibility, and even further that you have invited everyone right up to the Archbishop of Canterbury to participate in the wedding party, then the bridal table would look something like this: everyone is seated on one side, facing the guests, with the bride and groom in the middle and the cake between them. Facing the table, the bride is on the left, on her left is the best man, on his left is the groom's mother, then the bride's father, then a bridesmaid, then an usher. On the right of the cake is the groom, maid of honor, groom's father, bride's mother, usher, bridesmaid, etc. The clergyman sits at one end of the table, Archbishop or not. And your children may also be included, if they're old enough.

If you decide to seat your parents at their own table instead, then the arrangement should be bride's mother, groom's father, groom's mother, clergyman—reading counterclockwise. The bride's parents in this seating plan occupy the places of honor at opposite ends of the table, but if you feel it would be more appropriate to eliminate any such implied caste ratings, ask for a circular table. If the reception is small enough, however, there is no reason not to seat the entire party at one long table.

You may have place cards for your guests if you want, but most receptions are less structured, with friends and relatives deciding where they want to sit once they've seen who else is there. Still, such cards are usually set out for the bridal table, and for the parents' table if there is one.

FOOD AND DRINK

The only essentials at a reception are a cake and something with which to propose a toast. That something is usually champagne, but you can certainly have a dry wedding as well. Other drinks may include anything from cider, soft drinks, and lemonade right on up to full bar service, depending on your inclination, local custom, the time of day, and your budget.

As for the cake, the light pound and sponge varieties are popular, or even a rich fruit cake (called a groom's cake)—though this is a rarity at second weddings. The icing, as mentioned earlier, should not be all white for the same reason that the wedding dress at a second marriage is never all white. Pastels make a nice border and add the necessary color, or can be used on the base icing with white roses or borders.

The cake is always cut into many pieces so the guests can eat some there and take some home as well. The romantic legend says that unmarried girls will dream of their future husbands if they place a piece of wedding cake under their pillows. You should plan the size of the cake accordingly.

Other food is entirely your option, again depending on time of day, your budget, etc. Exactly the same rules that pertain to any other party should govern your decision here: do you want to serve a breakfast, brunch, luncheon, buffet, hors d'oeuvres, dinner, banquet, or nothing at all? How elegantly the food is served, and how extravagant the menu, are all part of how elaborate an affair you envision. One good rule of thumb to govern your decision here as elsewhere in second weddings is: *don't overdo.*

If you decide not to have a bridal table—usually because you are not going to serve any other food—then the wedding cake will occupy a table by itself, placed conveniently to traffic flow so that people will have easy access. The table should have a pastel cloth, and you may embellish it with a few flowers, if you wish.

The cake is cut first by the bride and groom, with the man's hand over the woman's on the handle of the knife. You share the first piece to demonstrate future parity, then back off and let someone else—usually a professional caterer—cut up the rest for the guests.

Generally the toasts precede the cutting of the cake, and these are always led off by the best man. The groom goes next with a tribute to the bride (and an acknowledgment of the best man's wishes), followed by the ushers and then anyone else who feels sufficiently moved by the availability of a public platform. The bridal couple remains seated during all toasts, except when the groom rises to offer his own salute to the bride, or when other members of the wedding party are the recipients.

Following the toasts, the best man may read aloud any congratulatory letters or telegrams from absent friends or relatives, depending on the wishes of the bridal couple.

DANCING

Dancing is purely optional at second weddings; you may find it perfectly right, or for a variety of reasons it may seem inappropriate. The guideline in the choice is that many social relationships in the first wedding have changed or dissolved by the time you have divorced and remarried. The bride's dance with her father, for example, could easily decline from a touching ritual the first time to a possible embarrassment the second. But you certainly know your relationships with your family and friends, and the decision is entirely yours. If you think the traditional, ritualistic aspects of the dancing should be reduced, then it is not unreasonable to begin with one or two passes around the floor by the bride and groom, followed by any or all of the guests as they see fit.

One of the nice things about dancing is that it does give the kids a chance to join in again actively, and some of these photographs are sure to give you many happy memories in the years ahead.

Throwing Things (Bouquet, Garter, Rice)

You should try to have a bit of rice or a few rose petals on hand for the children, but otherwise this first-marriage tradition is usually omitted at second weddings. If you have any unmarried girls in the reception, you may want to toss your bouquet, but without turning it into a squeally production. Omit throwing a garter in any circumstances.

By the way, you will probably want to save one or two flowers from the bouquet to pin on your going-away dress.

❀

CHAPTER 6

Who Gets Asked, Who Gets Told

LISTS

For various reasons already cited, the second wedding is almost inevitably smaller than the first. This means a guest list usually limited to relatives and close friends. Developing the list is pretty much the same, whether it's your first wedding or your tenth: each partner sits down alone and decides who he wishes to ask, then the two of you get together for the task of sorting, weeding, and finalizing. First-marriage etiquette decrees that the parents of the respective principals make up the lists initially, but, of course, in practical fact this is almost always done with the active participation—or at least the assent—of the bride and groom. Because your parents will play a more limited role this time, you and your fiancé should handle the invitations and announcements. Certainly it would be appropriate to include your parents in reviewing the list as it evolves, but be sure you and your future partner retain full control over its final contents. Unless your parents are paying for the wedding—which ordinarily they would not be doing this time—they have no veto power.

Another good reason to check the final list with parents is that they might remember some friend or relative, such as Dutch aunts and uncles, godparents, or great aunt Zelda in the nursing home in Trenton. These people are unlikely to come, but perhaps you owe them the ritual of being made to feel included.

By no means should you hesitate to invite someone just because you asked them to the first wedding. Usually these are the very people who are most anxious to share in your happiness—especially if they worried over your suffering or loss when your first marriage came to an end, whether by death or divorce.

At the second marriage, guests are not expected to bring a gift. This does not rule it out, and in fact most guests will wish to provide some remembrance. But it does remove from both the guest and yourselves any onus that might otherwise attach to the invitation. (You remember the old ploy from the first wedding: invite the cousins in Honolulu and your college pal now working in Outer Mongolia; they'll never make it, but they're sure to send a gift.) This time, if you have some reason to invite a guest you feel is not likely to attend, make sure the reason serves the friend or relative at least as well as it serves you; if you expect anything more than warm feelings, you deserve to be disappointed.

The lists for wedding announcements can be as long as you like. They should include anyone you would like to tell. Again, ask both sets of parents for their input, and this time give them free rein. Your children may want to add the name of a friend or two, but explain to them that they should advise such friends personally rather than in writing; unless the children's friends are your friends as well—which isn't likely—they should not receive an announcement.

INVITATIONS

Formal, engraved invitations are seldom sent for a second wedding, unless it is the second wedding for the groom only and the first for the bride. There are some circumstances, however, where you may feel an engraved invitation is indicated, whether by local custom, family acceptance, religious convention, or some other reason. In such cases, the invitation should begin one of two ways:

If you are widowed:

> *Mr. and Mrs. Walter Byrd Hooper*
> *request the honor of your presence*
> *at the marriage of their daughter*
> *Patricia Ann Pettit*

If you are divorced:

> *Mr. and Mrs. Walter Byrd Hooper*
> *request the honor of your presence*
> *at the marriage of their daughter*
> *Patricia Hooper Pettit*

(In either case, the rest of the invitation follows the conventional format for first weddings.)

As you can see, the only difference is in the name of the bride: the invitation uses her first and middle *given* names if she has been divorced from that rascal Pettit, but uses her first name, maiden name, and married name if poor Pettit is deceased. In neither event is the bride identified as "Mrs."

If for some reason the bride chooses to issue the invitation herself (the two most common reasons are simple preference and the death of one or both parents), then the formal format would again be inappropriate.

Even where the invitation is informal, however, occasionally the communication goes out over the signature of the bride's mother. Here again, it's your choice:

Dear Clara,

George and I (Patricia and George, if mother is doing the honors) are being married at noon on April first in the Little Chapel in the Woods here in Oak Bluffs. Following the ceremony, there will be a small reception at our house (either give the address here or on the letterhead). We hope you will be with us to share the joy of the day.

Affectionately,
Patricia (or Patricia's mother)

Such informal invitations should be written by hand in black ink on your best paper.

If you decide you want the guest to attend only the reception, follow the same format without mentioning the ceremony itself.

Mr. and Mrs. Walter Byrd Hooper
request the honor of your presence
(or *the pleasure of your company*)
at the wedding reception for their daughter
(bride's name)
and
(groom's name)
etc.

Mailing time is usually two or three weeks before the ceremony, depending on the size of the affair and the distance of the recipients. Similarly, telephone calls should also be made at least two weeks in advance—although the handwritten note is favored.

ANNOUNCEMENTS

The protocol for announcements of second marriages involves the same basic choice as the invitations: either the bride's parents break the news or the bride and groom themselves do the honors. To some extent, it depends on how old you are, but the same human considerations discussed elsewhere pertain here as well. One easy way out is to let your jewelry store, stationer, or large department store handle the announcements for you—the better ones all have bridal consultants who can simplify the question of whose name should appear at the top.

Assuming you don't have access to such help, here's what it looks like one way:

Mr. and Mrs. Walter Byrd Hooper
have the honor of announcing
the marriage of their daughter
(the bride's name here is determined on the same basis as
on the invitation)
and
(groom's name)
etc.

And here it is if you yourselves decide to announce it:

Mrs. Patricia Hooper Pettit (bride's first name and both
maiden and married surnames)
and
Mr. Peter Dana
are pleased to announce their marriage
etc.

You may also wish to include "at home" cards to advise recipients where you will be living after the wedding.

A rather rigorous protocol pertains with regard to invitations and announcements if you decide to go formal. There is normally a tissue over the written or printed portion of the card to keep it from smudging, and the message is placed in an unsealed envelope. Any printer worth his salt knows exactly how all this is done, and there is no point in repeating any of it here. If you decide on a handwritten note, draft such an invitation or announcement first, then show it to your stationer for advice on the proper handling and paper. As rigid as these various conventions may be, they are not really yours to observe; instead, go to the expert who knows.

Announcements are usually mailed the day after the wedding. It's a task better entrusted to a reliable friend or relative—preferably the maid/matron of honor—than yourself. Otherwise, there is a good chance the announcements won't go out until you return from your honeymoon.

PUBLICITY

If you wish the press to carry an announcement of your second marriage, just offer the essential facts. These would naturally include the statement that "The bride's first marriage ended in divorce," or that "The bride is the widow of the late William Shakespeare." Otherwise, you should provide a somewhat leaner, more austere version of whatever you sent out the first time.

How much publicity you want is entirely personal. Some couples never send out announcements, while others seek coverage in the local dailies from Bar Harbor to Palm Beach. If you choose to advise the papers, you might also include a photograph taken at the wedding or the reception, though it's not really customary for a second wedding. If you're news, the papers may call you back for more details.

Typically, such announcements are usually headlined with the bride's name by her first marriage: Patricia Pettit Remarries. But don't expect as much space as you got the first time—society editors still have not swung unanimously to the view that practice makes perfect.

CHAPTER 7

❀

What to Wear

Everyone knows the second bride never wears white, which symbolizes virginity. (On hearing this, so the story goes, one first-time bride thought it over for a long time, then decided on a white dress "edged in beige.") The second time, any pale or pastel color is appropriate—even beige, which happens to be a favorite—with the material, style, and length appropriate to the type of wedding, time of year, and time of day.

Everyone else in the wedding party takes the cue from the bride's choice of dress.

If the wedding is semi-formal, the bride will probably select something half way between a traditional wedding gown and a street dress. This usually implies a rich material, not too vivid a color, and a choice of cuts from long gown, to long dress, to a stylish shorter dress. Of course, your gloves and shoes should complement the outfit, and the fabric should be consistent with the expected weather for that time of year. A bridal veil is as inappropriate as a rose in the teeth. You should eschew both. The bride may decide on a hat or small bridal headpiece, perhaps of flowers. Picture hats are romantic, and if you're tall enough you may be pleasantly surprised at how flattering they can be. Even if you decide not to wear flowers as a wreath (either on your hat or in the hair), then at least do consider them as a nosegay with ribbons—especially if you have opted for a country wedding.

Whether the bride wears a hat or flowers will influence the style of her hair. Accessories should be minimized; one good rule is to include nothing more than you need to meet the requirements of "something old, something new, something borrowed, something blue."

The bride's attendants dress in keeping with the style selected by the bride, but the color or tone of their dresses set the bride apart. Hats and gloves also follow the bridal option. And bouquets or corsages should be equally consistent: flowers are recommended, at least in some form, especially if there are young girls participating in the ceremony.

The mothers wear street dresses with matching accessories. Corsages are optional, but if elected it would be a thoughtful gesture if they were supplied by the bride and groom. Hats are at the discretion of the individual mother, conforming to church rules, conventions, and the size of the wedding.

The groom and other men in the bridal party usually wear dark business suits at a semi-formal wedding, with white shirts and conservative ties as well as black shoes and socks. This is not inflexible, however, and depending on the time of year—and also on what the female contingent is wearing—the males may choose white or light jackets, with pale shirts, black ties and trousers, black shoes and socks. Or they may wear white trousers with white shoes and socks, and the same pastel or beige jackets.

If the wedding is informal, everybody wears street attire, starting with the bride. Perhaps this means the same dress she'd have worn if the event were semi-formal, but it eliminates full-length skirts or formal gowns. For the men, their options remain more or less the same—but without tending toward anything that looks like either a dinner jacket, a tuxedo, or a rental outfit.

Probably there is no more symptomatic place for the changing mores and attitudes toward second marriages to demonstrate themselves than in the way people dress. At this writing, very few department stores or bridal consultants can show the second-timer anything other than a warmed-over version of the bridesmaid's outfit for her wedding gown. But that should all be changing dramatically and soon. Even now, there are some stores where bridal specialists provide real help.

But until the rest of the world catches up, it's safer to approach these specialists with at least a rudimentary concept of what you want to look like on the big day. And do be sure to have all the facts straight about the season, style, and size of your wedding. My own dress, designed by Priscilla of Boston, was that relative rarity made specifically for a second wedding. Others will appear as the demand mounts. Meanwhile, if you don't have a Priscilla, you might still seek out the services of a good seamstress—or even try it yourself, if you're handy with a needle and thread. You can save a few dollars, and you're certain to wind up with exactly the result you want.

❀

CHAPTER 8

The Ceremony, Step by Step

Because the wedding is a ritual which formalizes the most important relationship in your adult life, planning the exact content of that ritual can assume awesome proportions. It goes far beyond the usual question of whether to leave the word "obey" in the exchange of vows—it involves the basic issue of how seriously you view this new commitment, and how you feel about the life you will be sharing in the years ahead. At the very least, you want this ceremony to express that commitment and that feeling adequately. And it should signal a new beginning in the most positive sense—not simply a rewarming of the same hopes and promises mouthed by rote when you were younger, but an exchange that is deeply and exactly your own, that expresses the best you share and those potentials you jointly embrace. It should be *your* ceremony.

Institutions are right now in a state of flux, with history favoring the latecomer. There has probably not been a time since the age of chivalry that so favored the personalization of ritual. Compare the latitude you enjoy in planning this ceremony with the strictures you were forced to observe the last time. Regardless of your religion, churches today are more receptive to change in the customary wedding ritual. *So take pride in making your wedding more personal and more real this time than it was before.*

There are seven major phases of a wedding ceremony, and while you can make of them what you will, they still require careful choreography if the result is to be a pleasure for all concerned.

EVERYBODY SIT DOWN

As discussed earlier, the left side of the church is generally reserved for the bride's family and friends, and the right side for the groom's. The front pews are reserved in either case for immediate family: parents, children, brothers, and sisters. The ushers should be instructed accordingly, but it should also be made clear that such guidelines are not ironclad laws. If the church is filling unevenly—perhaps because the wedding is held in the bride's hometown and the groom's is far away—then the ushers should seat late arrivals on the right side to restore some balance.

In second weddings particularly, the overall seating plan should respond more to convenience and symmetry than to any social onus for conformity to rules. The real law should be this: avoid tensions or any situation that is likely to lead to hard feelings. Let people sit where they want if they express a preference.

ENTER THE BRIDAL PARTY

Let's assume a maximum cast; if there are fewer, the relative order of appearance remains the same. The clergyman comes first, entering from the sacristy or some side room of the church, followed by the best man and then the groom. The clergyman turns and looks down the aisle; the best man takes his position at the far right, with the groom nearly in front of the cleric. They, too, turn and face the guests. The processional starts down the aisle to the music you've selected for the occasion. The bride is on the arm of her sponsor or else alone. The party can march two abreast or in single file, whether or not the bride is accompanied. The processional begins on the left foot and everyone stays in step to the altar, the ushers leading.

The ushers preced the bridesmaids, allowing a certain amount of space between the two. Because the distance involved is often relatively short, you may decide that each member of the processional should wait until his predecessor has reached their destination before that member starts down the aisle. This would not be feasible in St. Patrick's Cathedral, but you're not going to get remarried in such an auspicious institution, and the timing may prove just right for the aisle you have set up in a small chapel or your home. If there is a flower girl, she would follow the maid/matron of honor.

So here's the order of the processional: ushers, bridesmaids, maid/matron of honor, flower girl, and then the bride on her sponsor's arm. Though most second brides enter alone.

At the altar, the ushers stand behind the best man, in front of the groom's parents. The bridesmaids take up a similar position on the other side of the altar and they, too, turn to face the arriving bride. If the father of the bride has brought her this far, he may now decide to take a seat in the first pew with other members of the bride's family; it is not uncommon for the bride's escort to stop short of giving her away in a second marriage, once she is safely down the aisle. The bride then takes her place beside the groom, with the maid/matron of honor and the flower girl at her immediate left.

Suppose you decide to go all out at the semi-formal level and have all the functionaries listed above. There would probably be no more than one clergyman (with the rare exception of a mixed second marriage in which clergy of both faiths participate in an ecumenical ceremony), a bride and groom, a best man and maid/matron of honor, two ushers and two bridesmaids—plus perhaps the bride or groom's daughter as flower girl.

Grand total, at most: eleven. Though for second marriage the average is about five.

PROMISES, PROMISES

The vows are important to your marriage. And it's becoming more and more common for couples joining in a second marriage to add, subtract, or in some way personalize this part of the service. Of course, you can leave things alone and still enjoy a ceremony that both of you are happy with. But the trend is to add special prayers (often of the bride or groom's composition), poems and other literary works, and to custom tailor the vows to this one event, never to be used again by anyone else. This time, the previously married bride and groom are cementing a part of themselves into the foundation of their marriage.

In solemnizing the marriage, there is more than the simple exchange of vows. Other popular sources for material include the Bible (especially the Song of Songs and 1 Corinthian 13), folk songs, T.S. Eliot, Kahlil Gibran, Shakespeare . . . it might range from Nietsche or Kierkegaard to Houseman or Kipling.

Many people write pieces of their own to welcome guests or as a benediction. In the last case, the couple may well include a very personal prayer at the end of the ceremony, expressing their joy and gratitude for the participation of family and friends in witnessing their public declaration of commitment. My husband and I did this, but in the form of a printed welcome to our guests. Our children distributed it on the pews prior to the service. Consequently, the congregation is drawn into the special feeling that you and your fiancé have created, and are made to feel a part of the unique and beautiful service which is to follow. Most of your guests have been to a good many weddings, and yours should not be "just another one." Of course, all these special touches should be prepared and worked out with your clergyman's explicit understanding and approval very early in the planning of your service. Last minute surprises do little to make a wedding memorable.

What you do at the altar beyond these simple guidelines depends on your religion, your particular church, the disposition and flexibility of your clergyman, the customs in your part of the country, and other elements beyond the scope of this book. Your clergyman will advise you of the balance of the service and in all likelihood provide you with an appropriate written guide. Be sure to seek his counsel early so as to plan wisely.

Exeunt Omnes

When whatever you do is done, the clergyman will probably congratulate you both and indicate that the ceremony is over. At this point the bride and groom may kiss each other chastely but with conviction at the altar, or simply turn toward the guests and begin the recessional. Some churches have rules against kissing, so be sure to settle this detail firmly in advance.

One method of leaving is simply to reverse the order in which you all entered—in which case the best man would exit by a side door, usually the same one by which he entered. The other method is for everyone to form pairs: bride and groom, best man and maid/matron of honor, then ushers and bridesmaids, arm in arm, as though you were about to file aboard the Ark. If you're going to go the second way, make sure everyone matches up; any last minute attrition among the ushers, for example, could destroy the balance.

THE ARRIVAL AND GETAWAY

The logistics of second marriage transportation are more complex than the first time around. For one thing, you probably won't have any chauffeur-driven limousines to take the party to and from the church. The alternative is careful planning as well as the enlistment of relatives and friends.

If you are staying with your parents just before the wedding, you might go to the church with them either in their car or your own. Other possibilities include the maid/matron of honor or a close friend. You may have made plans for the children to spend the big day with someone else—hopefully not—but if they are in the ceremony, you should bring them with you and make sure they are in the proper place along with the rest of the bridal party thirty minutes before the service starts.

All this may seem rather hectic, so it is well to plan for an early start. It is also your responsibility to see to the transportation of any attendants who are not riding in the same cars with either the bride or groom. This is not so complex, but it can turn into an awful mess if it isn't figured out thoroughly beforehand, with everyone advised accordingly.

The groom and best man will ordinarily drive to the church together. The ushers should leave at least ten minutes ahead of them in order to meet any early arrivals and take up their stations forty minutes before the service begins.

Don't worry about the old superstition of running into your mate before the ceremony: in second marriages it doesn't count. Of course, you'll ride away from the church together, unless the reception is to be held right there or within a short walk. In either event, you will still have to plan for transportation away from the reception when you leave on your wedding trip. If a car is required from the church, the best man should drive the bride and groom—with no one else in the car. The maid/matron of honor can take care of the children in the short time between church and reception, or they can be entrusted to a grandparent. Bridesmaids and ushers should make their own plans for getting to the reception —but again, these arrangements should be made in advance to avoid confusion.

How you get away from the reception depends on what happens to the car afterwards: are you just driving to the airport or is the car to be your transportation all the way? If it's the first; then the best man may be called on to chauffeur one last time—perhaps even returning the car to your house afterwards so it won't sit at the airport for the entire time you're gone.

REHEARSAL

Even if your wedding plans involve no more than a best man and a maid/matron of honor, you must hold a rehearsal. If time permits, it should be held forty-eight hours before the real thing to avoid unnecessary fatigue. But the facts of life often argue against such planning, so perhaps you'll have to settle on the day before the actual wedding. The usual rehearsal lasts only about half an hour, allowing for the clergyman to explain everyone's function and the sequence of events. The organist should be there if you plan music, and the children should also be on hand unless they are very small and have no role in the actual ceremony. The rehearsal is especially important to give the kids confidence, as well as answering any questions that may be worrying them. You should be especially patient and prepared to go over the series of events several times— but only if the children seem to want it. (If they do, there's no reason to keep the rest of the party at the rehearsal; the older members can go on along.)

The clergyman is in charge at the rehearsal. He won't read the actual ceremony on the dry run, but he will advise everyone on his or her cues and make sure all responses are proper and delivered with authority.

MUSIC

If you decide to have music at your service, you should make arrangements early. Certainly you'll want to engage an organist if the wedding ceremony is semi-formal, unless the facilities are too small to permit it. The choice of music is another area in which the pastor has final veto power, so be sure to discuss your selections well enough in advance. The best way to engage an organist is through either the clergyman or his sexton, so the person they recommend will probably be familiar with the conventions and restrictions of that particular church or chapel.

If you are not married in a church—or if your wedding is nonreligious—you may want to consider secular music for the occasion. This is another area where the rules are fast changing, so consult whomever is in charge. For even in a church these days, your choices are not always limited to organ music. Clerics are aware that much of today's sacred music originated in the secular media, so they may be flexible about music considered popular if you can make a case for its use in church. Of course the most famous piece of wedding music ever written—the Bridal Chorus, or Wedding March—originated in Wagner's *Lohengrin*. Your organist should have some good ideas for something different since *Lohengrin* has become rather familiar with the passage of time.

Music for the reception is covered in Chapter 5.

❀

CHAPTER 9

Miscellany—Flowers, Photos, Guests, Gifts

FLOWERS

Flowers are a perfect symbol for festivity, and should be an important feature of your second wedding just as they were in the first. They go a long way toward dressing up an otherwise drab setting and even if the church or chapel is just exactly right, they're bound to improve the background for the reception. And by all means include them in the church as well; some things can become more perfect.

However, there are two caveats for the second-time bride to observe in her choice of floral arrangements. First, remember that you are no longer in a position to overdo with respect to white. This doesn't mean eliminating white flowers entirely, but you should be certain that there is a variation of color, if only the subtlest pastel, in everything from your bouquet to the arrangements on the altar. Virtue and virginity have only the most tenuous relationships in any circumstance, and in a second wedding there is no correlation whatever, but

don't forget that white represents virginity in this particular context or you risk a few raised eyebrows, snick-
ers, or worse.

The second constraint is simply don't overdo. Period.
Here again, the safest rule for a second-time bride is too
little rather than too much.

The best source for information on bouquets and
arrangements is, of course, your professional florist.
Flowers are no longer as subject to season as they were
in the past, but he can guide you in a selection that re-
flects the time of year, the exact feel you want to achieve,
and contributes toward a unified overall effect. More
than likely he'll also be familiar from past experience
with the site of both the wedding and the reception and
will know what works best. Even if he has never done a
second wedding before (there's hardly a florist alive that
hasn't, but perhaps he may not have been told some of
the previous jobs were second-timers), he'll have lots of
good advice. Make sure he knows what everyone will be
wearing, plus any other relevant details that will bear on
the size and color of the bouquets; big bouquets look
ludicrous in the hands of small girls, for example, and
the converse is equally disastrous. Shape and color can
be a problem unless the florist has all the facts in advance.

The bride's bouquet sets the tone for the rest of the
attendants. Her maid/matron of honor may have a con-
trasting or complementary choice of flowers, but in no
case should it outshine the bride's. Again, what's appro-

priate often depends on the time of year—violets look better in the spring, for example, while chrysanthemums are identified with fall.

Because this wedding is not formal, there are two places where you would definitely not use flowers: on the pews, and strewn in the aisle along the bride's path. However, you may mark the first pew only, for the mothers.

Instead of a bouquet, brides at second weddings often prefer simply to wear a corsage. If the wedding is semi-formal you may want a corsage anyway for your going-away dress, even though you carry a bouquet through the ceremony. Of course, you can't throw your bouquet if you decide on a corsage, which may be just another reason to elect the corsage depending on your age and the composition of the wedding party. Or at semi-formal affairs, the bride may settle on a flower-covered prayer book instead.

Probably you'll also want a corsage for each mother as well as grandmother, if they're present. Ladies' preferences should be asked; my own mother, for example, chose gardenias for the scent—but some people are allergic to them or may have other favorites.

The girls in the wedding party, including the bride, may also decide on floral headpieces. But here again, be careful not to get carried away.

If the bride decides on a bouquet, that determines what the groom wears in his left lapel. If not, then the common choices are lily of the valley or stephanotis. The best man's boutonniere may be the same flower or something reasonably close in appearance. The traditional lapel flower for the ushers and the fathers is a white carnation.

Don't overdo the altar or reception decorations either. Plan to have a few arrangements in the church, but no more than that. You have lots more latitude at the reception, yet take the advice of the florist on spotting the area with color rather than overwhelming everyone in sight with a sea of petals and perfume.

PHOTOGRAPHS

Snapshots are one way to make the day last as long as the marriage. This is a new beginning just as much as any first wedding, and its moods and colors and faces should be preserved permanently. Especially if children are involved.

Photographers often cost money, however, and this may be an important consideration. There are two ways to deal with the problem. The first is to shop around: prices vary enormously, and a high fee is no guarantee of high quality. The second is to ask two or three competent relatives or friends to cover the wedding with their cameras. Though beware of two things: You may encounter difficulty in obtaining the pictures when you return from the honeymoon. And also there is completeness of coverage—relatives and friends are not likely to have the push of a professional in recording the best moments, particularly if it means moving around inside the church or chapel. If you choose friends over the professional, offer to pay for the costs of their materials and processing. They may not let you, but you owe them that option.

This time around you will most likely dispense with the formal portrait. Such a studio shot is time-consuming, expensive, and has little or no use. If you want this type of picture for your own records, have it taken on the day of the wedding by your candids. Then even if you decide to offer it to the newspapers which is not recommended—though you may send written information—you can do it just as appropriately after the wedding as before.

The most important photographs you will get are the candids, especially those of the guests. Pictures of the wedding itself are fun to look at but could be of almost anyone. The candids, where the subjects are reacting to each other and to the event, are going to warm your winters for the rest of your life. Make sure the photographer knows who is who, and that he's kept up to the minute on your plans. This way he can be in the right place at the right time.

GIFTS FROM GUESTS

These are entirely optional at a second wedding, although most guests will observe the same conventions that pertain at first weddings, particularly if the invitation includes a large reception. This time, however, gifts tend to be less lavish and more practical than before, making up in thoughtfulness what they lack in costliness. It is assumed that a woman who has been married before has everything she needs in the line of conventional, wedding-present type possessions. Also, the second-time bride does not register her patterns and preferences with stores, so the guest is left more to his own devices. And nothing is more utilitarian or practical than a check or gift certificate. However, cash is a gift more appropriately made by a relative or close friend. And such gifts, of course, should be made out to both the bride and groom, rather than in the name of the bride by her previous marriage.

If the bride needs certain specific items for her home which she feels would be proper gifts, there is nothing wrong with letting her mother, sister, or close friend spread the word among guests who may be fumbling for a suitable remembrance. But as in all else, discretion and good judgment are the watchwords.

Often, older couples who are invited to second weddings may choose to give something they have owned for a number of years that the bride or groom has admired in the past. Such a gesture has particular meaning for both the giver and recipient—and its significance is likely to endure.

While guests at second weddings have little obligation with respect to gifts, recipients of announcements only have no obligation whatever. However, all recipients of invitations owe you a response, whether they attend or not. And in those rare instances when formal invitations are sent, you should expect a formal reply. Only when the invitation is verbal should the reply be verbal as well. In any event, whether your invitation is by letter or by word, formal or informal, your guests owe you the courtesy of a prompt reply.

If they decide their obligation—or inclination—includes a gift as well, that's up to them.

What you do with the gift after receiving it is likely to be different the second time, as formal displays of goods are frowned upon, mainly because they imply some form of pressure on those who chose not to give. On the other hand, you'll certainly wish to acknowledge the generosity of those who were kind enough to send a remembrance. Besides an immediate note of thanks, you may want to provide a small side area where donors can view their offerings on display—but in some part of your home where it will not proclaim itself loudly to those who gave nothing. Under no circumstances should such a display be made at the reception, even if in your home.

Gifts to Members of the Wedding Party

These are an obligation of the bride and groom, with each responsible for his or her attendants. Here again, thoughtfulness is more important than cost. The bridesmaids' gifts should all be identical, but you may want to do something a little different for the maid/matron of honor, as well as the flower girl if you have one. Similarly, all ushers should receive the same remembrance, with the extra thought going to the best man. There is nothing wrong with having every wedding participant receive exactly the same gift, but you do have some options.

The gift can vary, but general usage favors some small token such as a monogrammed silver belt-buckle for the men, a pair of earrings for the women—items they can wear during the ceremony as well as later. Other thoughts include cigarette boxes, lighters, writing sets, money clips, pearls. You know your friends: what do you think they would appreciate most?

THE BRIDE'S AND GROOM'S GIFTS TO EACH OTHER

Such gifts are likely to be far more personal, probably more expensive, and—let's hope—of enduring sentimental value. But here again, decide for yourselves whether you wish to exchange gifts, or if you prefer to give yourselves a joint present which you both select and both pay for. But whatever you decide, don't forget that the real gift you are making to each other is yourselves, and all the rest counts for naught.

Members of the wedding don't owe you any more than verbal thanks for the token you provide them. But every gift you receive from your guests requires an immediate response. And "immediate" means immediately after you receive the gift.

CHAPTER 10

❀

The Day

A definite countdown schedule for the day of the wedding should be worked out ahead. The amount of time you may need will depend on the size of your wedding, the help you get at home, how far you are from the site of the ceremony, and how well you have planned.

If you're a parent, be sure to allow for child-related problems, unless you want to arrive nervous, ruffled, and out of breath. (You'll probably arrive so anyway, but good scheduling can keep it from showing.) Regardless of their noblest intentions, the children are going to create a series of hazards which must be met and overcome, just as they do on those mornings when you are not getting married. There will be last-minute runs to the bathroom, soiled pants, ripped something, a too-thirsty gulp of No-Cal dribbled down the front of a new outfit, hair that demands recombing at intervals which never exceed five minutes, and on and on. Decide how much time you'll need for every reasonable contingency, add another twenty minutes, and pray that you get to church on time.

COUNTDOWN

MORNING

Good mornings start with a reasonable bedtime the night before. And one way to improve your chances of a sound sleep is to have a good friend or relative who'll take the children the night before the big day. If you have guests staying with you in your home (perhaps they came from out of town for the wedding), you should be wise enough to know when to stop entertaining—don't be shy about it. Should they not volunteer, depending of course on their age and condition, simply ask them if they would be willing to get breakfast for themselves and the children so that you can sleep. After all, their day will probably end before yours, especially if you plan any travel after the reception, and that extra hour in bed can make a big difference. Most friends or relatives will welcome such an opportunity to help. In any event, don't go to the other extreme and drag yourself to the kitchen at the crack of dawn to prepare a mini-banquet.

FIRST FOOD, THEN BEAUTY

After breakfast, look in the mirror. Not such a big item for grooms, of course, but this chapter is written mainly for the bride. If you had your hair done the day before, check to see if you need any touch-ups. You might want to go to the salon for a few minutes and have it combed out again. Whichever you choose—doing it yourself or having a professional do it—be sure to allow enough time. Damp, limp hair will spoil your day, and if your appointment runs late at the hairdresser you'll arrive home nervous, tense, and with your whole schedule badly out of whack.

PACKING REVIEW

Make a last-minute check of your packing, adding those few items that couldn't be included the night before. See to it that everything is ready to go when you are: suitcases, camera (with film), and any extra sporting equipment you may not find where you're going. Have everything right beside the door.

THE CHILDREN

Schedule a final review with the babysitter, regardless of whether a relative, friend, or someone you hired for the time you'll be gone. If the children will be staying with someone else in another house, plan to go through a checklist of the clothes and other things they'll need in your absence, and make sure they're all properly packed. *But:* don't put the kids' suitcases on the same side of the door as your own. If you do, you run the risk of honeymooning in a catcher's mask while your son snorkles blissfully with your new footfins.

WHEN IN DOUBT, SLEEP

After you've laid out the clothes and everything is under control, take two hours for a last touch of hedonism. Nap if you can, or take a nice, relaxing bath, pampering yourself with all the luxuries of bath oils, masks, and whatever makes you feel best. You want to be every bit as feminine and beautiful as you've ever been—with this time the advantage that you're a mature woman. Let it all come shining through. The only way to be truly vital and interesting is to feel that way within yourself.

DON'T TRY TO BE A FIRST-TIME BRIDE

This time, you have nothing to blush about, and no reason to simper or act demurely girlish. Let the difference show. When applying your makeup, for example, take it easy. You're not twenty now, so don't try to be. Too much rouge, heavy eye-liner, mascara and shadow, or too red a blusher will harden your looks. Unless yours is a night time wedding, very subtle colors are best, applied with a temperate hand.

DRESSING

You should start about an hour and a half before the ceremony. If there are children, get them dressed first and sit them down with a special book, puzzle, or particular toy saved for this occasion; whatever the ploy, it should be guaranteed to keep them moderately neat, clean, and distracted for at least forty-five minutes, while you continue dressing. If your maid/matron of honor can be there at the time, dressed, she may be able either to help you get ready or assist in preparing the kids. If you decide to dress at the church instead, you should plan to arrive there about ninety minutes before the service.

ONE HOUR AND COUNTING

By now, any other bridal attendants should also be at your house, dressed and ready to distribute the flowers (which should have been delivered shortly before their arrival). If the groom has children, you may plan for him to drop them off earlier so you can oversee their preparations. Fathers are famous for virtues other than their alertness in noticing such details as dirty fingernails, snarled hair, unmatched socks, and the wrong shoes. It would perhaps make sense to have all the children's outfits assembled at your house the night before, ready for their arrival and dressing under your watchful eye. (But take care not to offend the groom's mother, who may feel this is her big chance for a contribution to the smooth flow of events. Welcome such an offer if it comes.)

FORTY-FIVE MINUTES

The ushers should arrive at the church and put on their boutonnieres, which have been delivered by the florist directly to the church or picked up by the best man at the bride's house. (If there are *any* flowers sent to the church, as there are almost certain to be, then the

boutonnieres should of course be among them.) Properly
bedecked, the ushers then await the arrival of the first
guests in the church vestibule. If any of your children
are ushers, have someone deliver them to the church no
more than thirty minutes before the ceremony. This way
they won't suffer from excess itchiness. Again, the best
man is the logical candidate.

THIRTY MINUTES

At this point the organist begins the introductory music, assuming that's your choice. Guests arrive and are
escorted to their seats. The bride and her attendants pose
for last-minute pictures outside her home and then leave
for the church. Make sure that all ladies in the party
have whatever they need: at least a small purse containing the repair kit for last-minute touch-ups, and probably flowers, gloves, and headpieces as well. All children
report to the bathroom one final time, whether they say
they need to or not. (Make sure there is a bathroom at
or near the church for those who may have left early.)

TWENTY

The groom arrives at the sacristy with his best man.
The cleric will be there already—don't worry about *his*
schedule, he's been through it before. The marriage license is inspected for legal purposes, the best man con-
veys the clergyman's payment in the prescribed manner,
and last-minute instructions or reviews take place.

TEN

The bride appears in the vestibule. (If you don't already know, the vestibule is the area behind the pews, often a separate room, at the entrance to the church, while the sacristy is at the other end of the building, usually behind or beside the altar.) The bride, her attendants, and both sets of parents wait for the last arrivals to be seated.

FIVE

The groom's mother is shown to her seat in the right front pew, with the father following a few feet behind the usher. She enters the pew first, so the father is seated on the aisle.

TWO

The bride's parents enter in the same manner. But the mother makes the trip without her husband, of course, if the bride's father is going to give her away or simply escort his daughter in the processional.

GO

The music signals the beginning of the processional. Take a deep breath and smile. Remember, if you're crazy about ceremony, this is your big number. And if you're not, you can take pleasure from the certainty that you'll never be going through all this again.

✿

CHAPTER 11

The Getaway

Have you ever heard of anyone who chose his wife because she had a "bundle"? It works both ways, of course, and women make that decision as often as men. At one time, the French had institutionalized the marriage-for-profit concept to such an extent that it survives today in the form of our word, "trousseau," which is literally "bundle." But the French knew enough about the practical side of love to recognize that things go smoother when the marriage has a head start, such as a bundle of possessions—usually clothes—which the bride brought with her to see her through at least the first year of marriage. The concepts of a trousseau and a dowry are closely related. Dowry, by the way, traces back through Middle English and French to Latin, so both ideas have been with us a long time.

What has this to do with you? If you want your own marriage to get off to a smooth start, be sure to give the proper thought to the clothes you take on your honeymoon. Which means not only those you will wear when you get there, from snowshoes to swimsuits, but also the clothes you will need in transit both directions.

Once you and your fiancé have made a final decision about where to go on the wedding trip, find out what the weather will be like at that time of year and start planning accordingly. Your first and most important selection should be the going-away outfit. It must be practical and appropriate for both the trip and your destination. Chances are you won't go overboard with your trousseau this time for at least two reasons: you undoubtedly have more clothes than when you were married before; and probably this time you're going to have to pay for new acquisitions out of your own pocket. This second wedding is likely to cost enough without the addition of a whole year's supply of clothes. Usually the second-time bride buys conservatively and in moderation, selecting outfits that can mix and match and that can be worn afterwards to work or around the house. Start well ahead if you can, and pick up an item a week; then you won't notice the pinch as badly, and the little ones won't have to attend the ceremony barefoot.

Once you finish assembling the things you want to take along, pack with extreme care. Start with those items that won't wrinkle. But have everything else ready to go—back from the cleaner, freshly laundered and ironed, hanging by the suitcases, all set to be packed the day before the ceremony. An alternative to placing the luggage beside the door, suggested earlier, is to put everything in your fiancé's car the night before. Or the best man's car, if a practical alternative. The only thing you save for the last moment is a small train case containing those items you'll need right up to the end. Practical jokes aren't in perfect taste at a second wedding, but they still happen. A favorite target is the wedding couple's luggage. Careful planning, however, can avert embarrassment, inconvenience, and even occasional disaster.

Make a list of everything you need, and check it one last time when you pack. It's easy to forget something important. If you plan to visit a foreign country the resulting inconvenience can be especially costly since the price of simple items such as camera film, a tooth brush, or underwear can be much more expensive than at home.

The best laid plans—and the best thought-out lists—can be fallible, of course. Which can prove infuriating. So be thorough, leave as little as possible until the last minute, and allow nothing to chance.

As an aid to planning, here's a checklist you may find helpful in organizing both the trip and the exit.

1. If you have children, line up a babysitter the minute your honeymoon dates are confirmed; often they are hard to get for long periods, especially in the summer.

2. Plan to have everything you will need for the sitter and children done ahead of time; shop, pack for them, clean, stock the fridge early in the week so you can concentrate on yourself the last few days.

3. Make early boarding arrangements for any pets also. I've known two second-time brides who've sent the children to their grandmother's then spent the last two hours before they were married running around the

neighborhood, begging everyone they met to feed the cat and walk the dog while they were gone.

4. Decide what car to use for your getaway and see that it is tuned, gassed, clean, and at the place of departure when needed.

5. If you can, pack both your suitcases the night before or early the wedding morning; then put them in the getaway car so you won't have to worry about when to carry them out or how to pick them up after the service.

6. If your children go to the reception, make sure they know who is to take them home after you have made your exit.

7. If the men's outfits are rented, appoint someone to pick them up after the reception and return them the next day.

As a second-time bride, you may properly feel a bit foolish making a mad dash to the getaway car through a shower of rice and confetti. But don't count on getting away without it! Most of us try playing down the exit bit, explaining that this is just a party and we should all leave together, guests and bride and groom—but no such luck. The guests will stay as long as you do, will want to see you off together, and wish you good luck. You must honor this tradition—but you can deemphasize it somewhat.

For example, you don't have to supply the guests with the rice and confetti as is usually done in most first-wedding receptions. Some people, especially the children, will bring them anyway. This tradition is a token not only of fertility but of plenty, so welcome their good wishes.

When you feel it is time to leave and you plan to change, you may, if you wish, throw your bouquet. Many second brides prefer to give it to someone special rather than make a thing of it. Chances are, there will be fewer elegible young women at this wedding than at the first, so do as you feel best for the size and composition of the reception.

The garter is never thrown at a second wedding. For brides even to wear one the second time is considered frivolous by many. Also the idea of wearing blue, a color associated with the Virgin Mary (and, hence, purity) is inappropriate as well.

If you don't plan to change, you may elect to throw your bouquet just before you leave. Be sure to remember to remove one flower for posterity, or to wear as a corsage on your going-away outfit. Any stairway or high place such as porch or front steps is a good spot to do the throwing.

If you do change, your maid/matron of honor should accompany you to help in any way she can. In particular, she should see that your wedding dress arrives home from the reception if you don't plan to take it with you.

When you and your groom are ready, you should see your children and parents for private good-byes. It may be a difficult moment, especially for young children, but it's cavalier at least and at worst very cruel to run off without reinforcing your love for them, your thanks for their help, and the promise that you *will* return. Or, perhaps you're taking them with you—it's been done before. Our favorite photo in the whole album is the last one which shows a decorated station wagon (done by our children) going down the driveway with four little laughing faces and eight waving arms above the large "Just Married" sign. In our case, we chose this method to take the children home and see that they were settled with the sitter; we all said our goodbyes there. This way we could also change and pick up our bags at the same time.

When at last you are off, with your apprehensions and anxieties behind you, reflect on this very special day—so different from anything you have known in the past or will ever do in the future. This is the beginning of the happiness you were both once afraid you would never find. And whether your wedding ceremony was a simple, informal family service or a lovely semi-formal affair, it marks the start of a life that truly is "better the second time around."

CHAPTER 12

❀

Pitfalls

Unlike your first engagement period, this time you may be faced with some unusual problems. I don't pretend to be a psychiatrist, but there are certain situations that should be mentioned somewhere in this book, along with solutions that have worked for others in similar positions.

TELLING YOUR EX

If your previous marriage ended in divorce and there were children or alimony payments, you will have to inform your former husband of your plans to remarry.

If payments were sizable, your news will probably come as a happy surprise. Drop him a brief note stating the facts and the date of your marriage. Avoid the temptation to toss in a few barbs, or labor the point of finally finding happiness. This note should be written at least two weeks before the ceremony if you receive your payments weekly, or a month before if you are paid that way. Depending on your present relationship, you may even want to give him a call.

Regardless how amicably you parted, don't underestimate your ex's desire to avoid giving you one penny more than you have coming. If you are paid monthly, and you are to be married in the middle of the month, cash his check early, and rebate to him the part of the month that follows your wedding, sending it along with your announcement. This will save any embarrassment upon your return from the honeymoon.

If your ex is the jealous type or likely to unsettle you during this period, you can merely send an announcement after the wedding, returning any overpayment at that time. Though if there are children from the previous marriage, you should certainly tell your first husband of your intentions ahead of time. After all, he has a right to know about the man who will be a stepfather to his children, how they get along, where you will be living, and other plans affecting their lives. If he wishes, and the children want to, he may even take the kids while you honeymoon. This would not only save the expense of a sitter, but you'll know they are with someone who loves them during a time when they might feel just the least bit homesick and lonesome for Mother.

The Wicked Stepmother—You!

Every bride of a man with children by a previous marriage, whether they live with him or only visit occasionally, worries about being thought of as the shrewish old witch taking their father away from them—especially if they're young girls who worship their dad. There may be another strike against you too: their mother may not have painted a very pretty picture of you, so it will take time and patience on your part for them to realize that you really don't cluck over boiling pots.

One major word of warning, though: don't come on too strong. Children are turned off by adults who seem to trying to win them over with gifts and gushiness. On the other hand, don't go so far in the other direction that you ignore them or act as if you wished they weren't there. Let the children continue to share—perhaps more than before—in their dad's attention and love. At the outset you might do well to be restrained in sharing displays of mutual affection. Let them sense the warmth between the two of you but not so much that they'll feel threatened with exclusion. And do resist the temptation to hug or otherwise be physical with them, unless they're very young. Older children hate it and are terribly embarrassed. There are other ways to show you care.

Here are a few suggestions:

1. Make a place for them that's theirs. They will enjoy coming to visit if they know there is a spot that belongs exclusively to them. If you have an extra bedroom in your new home, fix it up with them the way they would like it. This is a good project for you all to work together on, and chances are they will love it and feel important and wanted. If a separate room all to themselves is impossible, try to work out an area or part

of a room they can share, perhaps with one of your children if they get along well.

2. Let them know you want them to come often. Give a small party in their honor. This is an especially good idea if they were unable to attend the wedding festivities. In this way you and their father will let them know what an important part of this newly formed bigger family you feel they are and how happy you are to have them. Let them know you want them to visit and share with you as often as they can. Consult with them on when they would like to come and what would be most fun for all of you. On big holidays, regardless of your husband's and your own wishes, they will probably not want to leave their home for yours, no matter how nice you make it. Don't be hurt. I never knew a youngster yet—or many adults for that matter—who wanted to be anywhere but home on Christmas. For children this also includes birthdays, Halloween, Easter, and occasionally Thanksgiving and the 4th of July.

3. Buy or keep something special that is theirs to have and use only at your place. They'll look forward to it each time, particularly if it's something they cannot for some reason have at their own home. We have a friend who married a girl from the country and they had several acres of land plus a small barn. The husband's teen-aged daughter loved horses and lived with her mother in New York City. When he picked up an old riding school mare, his daughter practically moved in for good. Obviously, most of us cannot afford a horse, or find it

convenient to keep another dog for someone else, but how about a kitten, or a hamster, or even a fish tank? Other ideas that have been loved and enjoyed by visiting offspring include street hockey set-ups, a race car track, gas powered planes, Dad's old scooter, your old doll house, a trunk of your gowns for dress up or collections of anything. Use your imagination; it's fun and far better than buying them toys for no reason every time they come for a visit.

4. If they want to, and if your plans permit, try to involve them in the wedding; they will almost certainly enjoy being a part of the festivities and can thus experience the joy of this new unity and feel wanted, especially if they have some duty to perform. We outlined some of these ways the children could be involved previously.

5. Discover what interests them, even read up on it so you can talk together.

"You're Going to What?"

One of the most annoying things you may hear during your engagement and the first few months following your wedding is the occasional cry of horror and disbelief from some would-be friend when you say you're going to marry again. You may hear this indirectly or straight out from some callous types who just can't make the mental adjustment, even when it means you have found happiness. The first time you marry, nearly everyone is happy for you, but the second time you make the same announcement you may be surprised to find some people don't share your joy. Usually this is more often true for your fiancé than for yourself. Men, it seems, hate to see a buddy "take the gas" as they put it, especially after having been burned the first time. Usually there are two reasons for a negative reaction like this and you shouldn't be too upset.

1. Jealousy—A single person often hates to see another single give up this marvelous state for matrimony. He may actually be jealous that he does not have a deep, loving relationship with anyone and a future to share. Or perhaps his or her own marriage may be rocky and your happiness hurts too much for him to be happy for you.

2. "It's the thing to say"—After all, being single is the sublime state of existence, right? Wrong. But it's playing the game and it's the expected reaction today, particularly for men, to pretend that they don't want to be married a first time, let alone a second.

You will find the most outspoken critics of second marriage to be those who are unhappily married themselves or who have been through a difficult divorce. They find it hard to be joyous over your plans. Be stout of heart: there are ways to keep this from depressing you and your husband—especially since he will probably receive the brunt of it.

First of all, be completely confident, positive, and visibly happy in your response. Say, for example: "Yes, it's true, Bill and I are going (not "plan"—be more positive) to be married. We're both very happy and very much in love." This satisfies most female friends, though your fiancé may have to be a bit more direct with the critical masculine comments.

$$$—YOURS AND HIS

The commonest problem in most marriages is money, and this can be true for the second marriage probably to a greater degree than the first, since more is involved.

Perhaps it may have been one cause of your downfall the first time. In any event, couples planning to marry again should work out carefully all their finances well ahead of the wedding. This will avoid any unpleasant surprises later, and you'll both know where you stand, how much you need to live on, and who is going to assume responsibility for what.

Subjects that must be worked out include:

1. Your job. Whether you'll get one or, if you're working now, keep the one you have. I know a girl who broke her engagement over this issue. She liked the feeling of independence acquired after her divorce and the satisfaction in doing something other than changing diapers. She enjoyed getting out into the world, meeting people, and keeping her mind active, and also liked knowing that if she wanted a new dress it was possible to go out and get it without having to account to anybody. Her fiancé insisted she give up her career and spend her days in front of a stove instead of a typewriter.

She was surprised at his stubborn insistence and his failure to understand her needs and avoided another possible disastrous marriage in time by talking out all these issue in advance.

2. Where will you live? His place, yours, or a completely new location?

3. Who pays for what? Make a list and budget of all money items. Decide what you will do to help out and what he can pay for that you have been previously. Be sure you are open, with no secrets to surface later and embarrass you. A lie about money is no beginning for an honest relationship.

4. Separate checks. Frequently each partner may wish to remain partially independent financially, and this is understandable. After living alone for a period of time the woman especially has become accustomed to managing on her own; for perhaps the first time in her life she may have actually found she is capable of handling her own finances. She is aware and cautious, a better planner, shopper, and economizer. Many women feel it's unfair to give up a small personal account in checking and/or savings. If either partner was "burned" in the dissolution of the first marriage, he or she may need this extra security. It is also useful where child support payments may be numerous and the money coming in and going out must be monitored carefully for taxes, education, older college-age children, etc.

5. Alimony. You will, of course, be giving up this income and must plan either on getting along on your new

husband's salary or taking a part-time job to supplement his income.

6. Child support. When you're laying your cards on the table, be sure to include an open discussion of how much weekly or monthly support you receive for your brood. He will also disclose what he sends out to his children. If there is a large difference here either due to a disparity in number, ages, or sex of the children or financial background differences, it is best to realize this ahead of time so that there will be no hard feelings later on.

IN-LAWS, ESPECIALLY HIS!

As we mentioned in the engagement chapter, parents may be a bit more of a problem this time than during your first marriage. It is not surprising that you will be viewed as a possible threat to their son's happiness; after all, they don't want to see him miserable again.

The same approach applies in dealing with parents as with the children. You can't force your friendship on them, but will just have to be patient; with a little effort in the right direction, and time, it will come. Be sincere, friendly, considerate, and warm. If someone genuinely likes you and is openhearted and kind, you can't help being flattered. No one can dislike someone who thinks they're great. Other ideas for winning them over include:

1. Invite them often and cook their favorite meals.

2. Remember them on special occasions, holidays, birthdays, anniversaries, or when they're sick, with personal notes, calls, and cards—but nothing too gushy.

3. Compliment them often and sincerely, especially on their son.

4. Offer to help in any way you can and be openly grateful for any small favors from them.

5. Get them involved in your future plans and ask their opinions. Remember that with their experience they might just have some good ideas.

GUESTS WHO WANT TO STAY WITH YOU

Most second brides do not live with their parents. They may share an apartment or live in a small house. Often a close friend or relative coming from a distance for the wedding may assume that since you have a place of your own you could most certainly let them stay with you—it will save the cost of a motel room, and would be much more fun. Only for them, that is, but not you.

The decision is all yours, of course, and perhaps you have plenty of room and lots of help and like confusion. But my advice is to avoid it. You will be much too busy to be a proper host and need as much rest as possible before the big day. Guests fail to realize that you are putting on the whole show yourself this time with little help from your parents. Plus, probably, you now have children and a daily routine to carry on in addition to the wedding plans. Having to shop and entertain guests is just too much. If a guest should actually invite himself, explain as nicely as possible your problem and suggest that you can make reservations at a place you think they'll find more peaceful than your madhouse. To make them feel they are not being too abruptly put off, plan to have them over for a tea or luncheon a few days before the wedding.

WE JUST CAN'T HAVE EVERYONE!

And in a second wedding this is definitely more true than before. Someone's feelings are bound to be hurt; you can't help it unless you plan a civil ceremony and no one gets invited. You will be forced to chose only close friends; those others who feel they should be included are going to be upset. About all you can say is "Sandy, Bill and I would love to have had you and many of our other friends at the wedding. You know second weddings are usually very small family affairs, but we plan to have a open house (dinner party or whatever) when we return from our honeymoon. We hope you'll be able to come."

"MUM, I DON'T WANT YOU TO GET MARRIED."

If one of the children doesn't want you to get married —or worse yet really doesn't like your future husband— you have a situation I fortunately didn't experience. However, if it is a serious emotional problem (and only you can judge this) professional help should be sought.

Many small children fear losing Mummy to this new man just prior to the wedding. You will, of course, find this upsetting, but it is not unusual. They've been used to having you pretty much to themselves and the thought of having to share you, coupled with a possible move to a new home, is a difficult adjustment for most children. Try to reassure the child as often as possible about how much better it will be for all of you when you are married. Tell them you will be a real family with two parents to love them instead of only one. If you have been working and will be able to give up your job, let them know you will now have more time for them and to do things together. And tell them frequently how much you love them and that they will ALWAYS be the most important people in the world to you, no matter what.

The mother–son and father–daughter jealousy is another common problem with children which usually works out with patience and time. Often a young son who has felt he was the man in the family since his father left will resent another man coming in and taking over as the male in the house and also as the man in his mother's life. Similarly, your daughter may feel no one can take the place of her dad who is the most special man in her life, and she may be upset with you for bringing someone else into the picture. She will still feel a strong loyalty to her real father and this is as it should be. Your best response to both these problems is not to try to push a relationship on them with their future stepfather. Let time work its course, along with patience and lots of love.

CHECK LIST

When you've made the decision:

— See your clergyman about the best time and any possible restrictions.
— Set the date.
— Discuss the wedding budget with your fiancé and/or parents.
— Choose the type of wedding most appropriate.
— Determine the place for the ceremony.
— Plan reception and make reservations if needed.
— Decide on attendants and ask them.
— Settle on a honeymoon site with fiancé.
— Begin looking for a sitter.
— Make your reservations *after* you get her, not before.
— Prepare your guest list.
— Start hunting for a dress.
— Plan where you will be living.
— Obtain any legal papers your divorced or widowed status may necessitate. *Don't leave this to the last minute.*
— Apply for passports and have innoculations (if required).
— Begin hand-written invitations.
— Order announcements.
— Shop for whatever you'll need for the big day as well as for your honeymoon.
— Discuss colors and dress style with mothers.

— Meet with fiancé and attendants to select proper dress for them.
— Choose children's wedding outfits.
— Line up a photographer (professional or otherwise).
— Discuss ceremony plans with clergy and others involved.
— Prepare any personalized portions of the service.
— Give above to clergyman for approval.
— Hand-address announcements.
— Go with fiancé to buy rings.

30 days:

— Mail invitations.
— Arrange receptions details.
— Order cake and flowers.
— Buy gifts for attendants as well as each other.
— Have fitting for dress and headpiece.
— Arrange lodging for guests.
— Schedule rehearsal and make rehearsal dinner plans (if you are to have one).
— Write thank-you notes for any gifts.

Two weeks:

— Confirm baby sitter.
— Complete wedding and honeymoon attire.
— Get marriage license.
— Settle transport to wedding service (and point of departure for honeymoon).
— Schedule hairdresser appointment.

One week:

— Pick up all clothes and rented accessories.
— Begin packing for honeymoon.
— Make lists for sitter of children's routine.
— Stock food as well as other necessities for brood and sitter.
— Make arrangements for any pets.
— Get kids ready: haircuts, clean clothes, etc.
— Have announcements ready to mail.
— Check reception plans.
— Inform wedding party of rehearsal time and routine.
— Drop your ex a note or have it ready to mail the day after.
— If stepchildren are in wedding see things are in order for them also, preferably in your care.

Final:

— Check on flowers, music, photographer, etc.

Now turn to "The Day," page 99.